# COUNTRYSIDE
# RAMBLES

# COUNTRYSIDE RAMBLES

by

*W. S. Furneaux*

YESTERDAY'S CLASSICS

ITHACA, NEW YORK

This edition, first published in 2019 by Yesterday's Classics, an imprint of Yesterday's Classics, LLC, is an unabridged republication of the text originally published by George Philip & Son Ltd. in 1920. For the complete listing of the books that are published by Yesterday's Classics, please visit www.yesterdaysclassics.com. Yesterday's Classics is the publishing arm of Gateway to the Classics which presents the complete text of hundreds of classic books for children at www.gatewaytotheclassics.com.

ISBN: 978-1-63334-046-6

Yesterday's Classics, LLC
PO Box 339
Ithaca, NY 14851

# PREFACE

HIS little book is an attempt to help those who are interested in the works of Nature by calling attention to many of the more striking objects and phenomena which reveal themselves to the country rambler. So many subjects are dealt with that individual descriptions are necessarily very brief and imperfect, but the object of the work is not so much to supply detailed information for home reading as to arouse an increased desire to study the beauties and wonders of the countryside— to encourage a careful observation of the former and an independent investigation of the latter. Doubtless much pleasure and profit are to be gained by the mere reading of Nature's wonderful works, but such advantages are not to be compared with the intense pleasure and satisfaction which rewards those who search out the beauties with their own eyes and attempt to solve the mysteries by their own efforts.

It is hoped that this little volume will lead many to take a living interest in their surroundings during their countryside rambles.

# CONTENTS

## *SPRING*

## *SUMMER*

## AUTUMN

## WINTER

# SPRING

# CHAPTER I

# THE AWAKENING
# OF NATURE

PRING is the season of the general awakening of Nature. During the cold months of late autumn and winter many of Nature's creatures have been in repose; but now, called forth by the gradually increasing power of the sun's rays, they resume their life of activity. Thus spring, with all its promises of renewed life and vigour, following a comparatively dull season of chilly sleep, is welcomed by all, but especially by the lover of Nature, who delights to watch the ever-increasing response to the call of the ascending sun.

The first signs of returning life are visible long before the winter is really over; for although the night frosts are still keen, and the atmosphere by day often very cold, yet the occasional intervals of bright sunshine arouse many slumberers from their necessary rest. So we find the hazel in full bloom, and often the yew, elm, alder, and other trees; while many of our favourite spring flowers lift their blossoms before the snows have ceased to fall. Many hibernating creatures, too, leave

1

their winter homes under the influence of a genial sun, perhaps only to return on the approach of another spell of wintry weather.

But with the real advent of spring new changes are to be witnessed every day. New vegetable growth appears in great abundance. The ground herbage shoots upward with astonishing rapidity, soon overtopping the dead stalks and leaves of the previous year. The trees and shrubs, one after another, are tipped with green as their bud-scales expand and reveal the tender leaves they enclosed; and new flowers are constantly appearing everywhere.

Some plants died to the roots before the winter set in, but not until they had scattered seeds for the perpetuation of their species; and now we see hundreds and thousands of their offspring thrusting their tiny leaves above the soil. Even the seeds of these plants must necessarily take their period of rest; and as some require a longer sleep than others, we find some of the seedlings appearing long after others have made a sturdy growth.

Many plants died down to the ground while the portions beneath the surface continued to live. Most of these laid up a store of food material in their stocks, tubers, bulbs, or creeping underground stems; and thus they are able to produce strong growths with great rapidity as soon as the temperature becomes favourable.

In woodlands it is interesting to watch the growth of seedling forest trees. Here we see hundreds, even thousands, of little beech trees, oaks, birches, ash, etc., just peeping above the soil; often so thickly placed that they could not possibly attain any great size; but they are exposed to so many dangers that, regardless of position, only a very small proportion are able to survive. In many cases these seedlings are far from their parent trees, but this is due to the fact that the seeds (or fruits) were so constructed that they were easily carried by the breeze, or that they were scattered by the agency of wild birds or quadrupeds.

As regards animal life, there are many creatures that do not spend the winter in repose, for they are able to obtain their natural food throughout the cold season. Thus the herbivorous rabbit can always find a meal of green food except when the ground is covered with snow, and then it will attack the bark of young trees; birds can nearly always obtain the seeds, berries, grubs, etc., which form their winter diet; and the carnivorous fox, stoat, and weasel seldom search in vain for their prey; but most of our other wild creatures are compelled to sleep through the cold season, either because their natural food is not to be found, or because they are unable to withstand the severe winter weather.

And now, in early spring, these creatures are aroused by the warm rays that have penetrated to their hiding-places, and one by one they reveal themselves to us as we take our rambles.

Frogs and toads return to their ponds while yet they may be imprisoned by a barrier of thick ice, and even on a frosty night their croakings fill the air. A bit later in the season the little hibernating and winter-hiding quadrupeds resume their active life. Soon we hear the familiar rustle of the little lizards as they rapidly dart away amongst the herbage of a sunny bank, and again observe the gliding movement of the snake as it rapidly seeks cover when we intrude in its haunts.

Then the air becomes more and more thickly peopled with insect life day by day. The very first warm and bright spell of sunshine entices the hibernating butterflies and other insects from their winter retreats, among them the queen wasps and wild bees which are, in most cases, the sole survivors of the large families of the previous summer. And as soon as the warmth of the sun has penetrated an inch or so into the soil, the numerous pupæ, which have escaped the ravages of insectivorous creatures, burst open their brittle cases and emerge with new-formed wings, soon filling the air with myriads of flies, butterflies, moths, and other denizens of the air.

These early insects soon find their mates, and it is not long before millions of tiny eggs give rise to as many little grubs which immediately commence their ravages on the new tender leaves and flowers of herbs and trees.

So, as the spring advances, fields, hedgerows, woodlands, and wild wastes teem with increasing animal and vegetable life, newly aroused from its winter sleep by the genial sun; and the air is filled with the soft hum of insect life, the twitterings and joy-peals of birds, and the sweet odours of opening flowers.

We ourselves are influenced by the warmth and brightness of this enchanting season, and we long to ramble over the countryside where freshness breathes and all sleeping things are brought to active life again.

# CHAPTER II

# OPENING BUDS

EW features of the spring attract more attention than the bursting of the buds on our forest trees and shrubs. In fact, the appearance of the little touches of delicate green on the tips and sides of twigs which, for several months, have revealed no outward signs of life, is often regarded as one of the principal indications of the opening of the season. And the general effect of these numerous patches of green, standing out in bold contrast with the sombre background, is so pleasing to the eye, and, withal, so full of promise, that one may well wander by hedgerows and through wood and copse with no other object than to enjoy an open view of the swelling verdure.

It is interesting, too, to note the varied tints of the new foliage of different trees, ranging from a very pale yellowish green to olive and bronze; to watch the rapid progress of the young leaves as they emerge from the grasp of the brown scales which have enclosed them since the previous summer; and to observe the order in which different species respond to the call of spring.

But we shall do more than this, for we wish to watch the gradual expanding of individual buds in order to see how the young leaves were folded so compactly in their winter homes; to observe them as they slowly expand; and to see the wonderful provisions made to shield the tender leaves from the dangers to which they are at first exposed.

To carry out such observations we must either pay frequent visits to the budding trees, or adopt some means by which we can watch the expansion of buds at home.

Very frequently we are able to find buds in various stages of development all on the same branch; and when this is the case we have a good opportunity of studying the history of the opening buds by passing our attention from one to another, in proper order. Thus you may often see a small twig of the beech tree bearing buds that show no signs of opening beyond the loosening of the outer brown scales, together with several others in which the young leaves have emerged and commenced to unfold.

But quite a large number of buds will open if the twigs bearing them are placed in water or wet sand, and these may be closely watched at home. Yet twigs selected for this purpose should not be cut too early in the season. Buds must have their natural period of rest; and it is best not to cut twigs for the purpose suggested until the loosening of the scales shows that the buds are ready to expand.

Among the buds that may be successfully treated

in this manner we may especially mention the horse-chestnut, beech, sycamore, poplar, and willow. But it must be remembered that there are limits to the growth of young leaves when treated in this way, for they are not supplied with their natural food. Yet the progress they make is quite sufficient for our present purpose, which is to see how the leaves are folded in the bud, and to watch them as they gradually assume their later forms and positions.

It is remarkable that the twigs of some trees, particularly those of poplars and willows, readily form roots when placed in a vessel of water; and these, if supplied with an ordinary mineral fertilizer, or transferred to damp soil, will soon develop into perfect, self-supporting trees; and their leaves will then grow to their full size.

Now let us examine some of the more interesting of the opening buds. To the left are some of the beech tree, in different stages. At first the overlapping brown scales which tightly embraced the embryo leaves gradually relax themselves; and, shortly after, a peculiar little mass of closely-folded leaves, covered with silky hair, protrudes at the tip.

*Opening Buds of the Beech*

When a little farther

8

advanced, we see that the young leaves, which are of a very light and delicate green colour, are folded in a manner that suggests the concertina, or the bellows of a photographic camera, that there is a vein at each projecting angle, and that the whole is protected by a dense covering of tiny hairs. Later still, each leaf widens, so that the veins are slightly separated, and the green tissue is rather more exposed. Even when the leaf has almost assumed its full size it still retains an indication of its former folds, and now we are aware that the silky hairs, which at first formed a complete covering, occupy the edges and the lower sides of the veins only, while the delicate green tissue between is bare and glossy.

Now let us see the reason for this. In the first place we must note that the space within the scales of the leaf-buds, not only of the beech, but of all our trees, is very limited, so that it is necessary for the little leaves within to be compactly folded, crumpled, or rolled. At the same time, the veins of these young leaves are always very prominent and well-formed, while the thin tissue between them is at present only slightly developed. This latter feature is a valuable protection to the leaves; for the thin skin or epidermis covering the blades of the leaves is, as yet, very thin, and not impermeable to water; and if there were a considerable surface of this imperfectly protected tissue, the young leaves would lose much of their moisture and die on dry sunny days. Further, all young leaves retain their folds, crinkles, or scrolls for a time after they have become free; for, in this condition, the thin substance between the veins, still covered with an exceedingly thin epidermis, is less exposed to sun and wind.

In the case of the opening buds of the beech, while the above conditions hold, there is a further protection against drying up afforded by the hairs. We have seen that these hairs exist only on the veins and margins of the young leaves; but at first, when the thin tissue is completely hidden within the folds, and the veins and margins only are exposed, the silky covering is complete. After the leaves have partially expanded, and the outer wall of the epidermis is becoming thicker, the covering of hairs, so necessary at first to shield them from dry winds, is now not so essential; and, later still, when the leaves are fully extended, and sufficiently protected by their perfectly-formed epidermis, the hairs, being no longer required, gradually fall, so that old beech leaves are quite or almost free from them.

The leaves of the hornbeam tree are very like those of the beech, with the same strong, parallel veins; and they are folded in the same manner within the bud, so that the above remarks apply also to them.

*Hornbeam*

If you examine the opening buds of our common forest trees, you will find that in several of them the young leaves are protected from sun and wind by a covering of hairs. Among them we may mention the white poplar, mountain ash, wild pear, and the wayfaring tree—a shrub rather than a tree, very common in the hedgerows of South England, more especially in chalky districts; and, as in the case of the beech, the hairs partially or entirely disappear as the leaves become older. The hairy coat of the last named (the wayfaring tree) reveals a wonderful structure when examined under the microscope; for each hair has several branches all radiating from one point, like the rays of a star, and the branches intermingle so thickly that they form a natural felt.

Some young leaves, not provided with a hairy coat, are protected against loss of moisture by a thin covering of natural varnish that is waterproof; but this, like the hairs, disappears when such protection is no longer necessary.

Again, some newly-exposed leaves, not protected or not sufficiently pro-tected by the means above mentioned, adopt curious devices for the prevention of loss of moisture. One interesting example will be seen in the young leaves of the horse-chestnut. These leaves are compound, each consisting of five

*Horse-Chestnut*

11

*Young Leaves of
the Horse-Chestnut*

or seven leaflets. As they first issue from the bud the leaflets stand erect and close together, thus sheltering one another from the sun.

Then, after becoming so long that this position is no longer possible, the leaflets sink, and hang perpendicularly with their points towards the ground. In this position they do not catch so many of the sun's rays. Finally, when the epidermis is well formed, and the light and heat of the sun become necessary for the functions the leaves have to perform, the leaflets rise and spread themselves horizontally. These precautions appear to be necessary even though the young leaves have a rather dense covering of woolly hair.

Another protective device will be observed in the young foliage of the wild cherry. Here the new leaves are folded only down the middle—along the midrib; and for a time they remain flatly folded in this manner, so that much of their surface is shielded from the sun.

A still more interesting example is afforded by the opening buds of the wayfaring tree already mentioned. When first the leaves appear they stand erect, as is the case with many other species, because in that position they are less exposed to the sun. At this time, too, they are much folded, and the veins are so strongly developed that they touch one another, completely hiding and protecting the deep folds of the green tissue between them. Then the leaves are also arranged in pairs, and are convex on the outer side, so that the margins of each pair fit closely together, form-

*Young Leaves of
the Wayfaring Tree*

ing a closed case round the growing apex of the new shoot.

In addition to all these protective measures, there is the thick, felted coat of hairs already mentioned covering the outer surfaces. As the leaves further develop, and the epidermis is well formed, the veins become farther apart, and the leaves lose their folds and take a horizontal position.

After observing a variety of opening buds we soon come to the conclusion that the so-called "leaf-buds" are really undeveloped branches, for each one eventually gives rise to a complete branch or twig. In many instances the branches bear flowers in addition to leaves, while some buds give flower-clusters only, or flowers with only a few scale-like leaves. We also learn that while some trees produce their leaves before their flowers, others, like the oak, bring forth leaves and flowers at the same time; and others, again, produce their flowers before their leaves, like the hazel, ash, elm, sloe, and some of the willows and poplars.

It may appear strange that some of our trees should produce their flowers so early in the year—often long before the winter is at an end; but there are various reasons why this should be so. In not a few instances the fruits ripen so slowly that the coming winter frosts would destroy them before they were mature if they had not a very early start. Again, the very early flowers that come before the leaves probably have a much better chance of being fertilized in the absence of foliage. If their pollen is distributed by the wind, they are so exposed to the breeze that the process is more likely to be successful; and even if they require the aid of insects it is probable that their prominence compensates for the comparatively small number of insects at present on the wing.

CHAPTER III

# THE REAPPEARANCE OF HIBERNATING CREATURES

HE genial warmth of early spring, which calls the young leaves from their winter homes, also entices numberless animal creatures from their respective hiding-places. But the latter do not, as a rule, attract so much attention as the bursting buds. They do not form a distinctive feature of the landscape, and are generally so shy or so skilfully hidden by their surroundings that they are not often seen except by those who search for them. Yet they are all exceedingly interesting; for, in addition to their varied forms and colourings, often really beautiful, they exhibit a variety of movements that render them especially attractive.

If you wish to make the acquaintance of these creatures you must be prepared to exercise some amount of patience, but you will seldom do so without reward. A noiseless saunter beside a sunny bank, the weedy border of a field, or along the edge of a wood or coppice, will often enable you to see a timid creature that would dart under cover at an abrupt intrusion. Or, remain quietly at rest in a favourable spot, and, sooner or later, some little animal will approach you so closely that you can observe its every movement. If you are previously acquainted with the haunts of certain creatures you wish to observe, so much the better; but, even without such knowledge, a careful selection of a post of observation will almost surely lead to success.

A few of the so-called hibernating animals are really only partial hibernators or winter hiders. These generally lay up a store of food for the cold season; and, awaking from their slumbers on a mild day, indulge in a meal and a certain amount of exercise. When, however, the frosts are all over, they commence a life of almost unbroken activity.

The squirrel is one of these partial hibernators. In very early spring you may see it—or, rather, them, for they generally live in pairs—running and leaping among the branches of trees, and occasionally descending to the ground to unearth some of the remains of their winter store. When the latter is exhausted, they will feed on young shoots, buds, and the bark of young branches until a fresh supply of nuts and beech-mast has ripened. All their movements are graceful and interesting; and if you approach their haunts cautiously, and remain quite still, they will proceed with their antics just as if unobserved. Before the spring is quite over they build their summer nest, usually in the fork of a tree, intertwining dead grass and thin twigs with moss and dead leaves. The whole mass so closely resembles the bark of the tree in colour that frequently the nest is scarcely noticeable from below. Here, in or about June, the female brings forth three or four blind and naked youngsters.

The pretty little dormouse, another partial hibernator, is just like a tiny squirrel in appearance, but its tail is not quite so bushy. Like the latter, it lives chiefly in trees, and feeds in a sitting posture on its haunches, holding its food between its hands; but it is chiefly nocturnal in its habits, so that it should be looked for in the evening at dusk. It has a beautiful tawny coat, against which the large black eyes are very conspicuous. Dormice leave their winter quarters permanently in late March or in April, and it is not long before they build their summer nests, either in underwood, two or three feet from the ground, or in a dense tuft of dead grass or other herbage. Towards the end of the present season you may see in each nest three or four young, blind and naked.

In fields and hedgebanks we may meet with another of the partial hibernators—the common field-mouse. This creature is very like the mouse which infests town houses, but is distinctly red-

*The Field-Mouse*

dish above, and whitish beneath. Its tail is about as long as head and body together. Although chiefly nocturnal in its habits, it is often at large in broad daylight. Frequently it spends the whole winter in country houses, or in barns, cornstacks and haystacks, and then does not appear to hibernate at all.

Now let us note the principal of the true hibernators, remembering that even these do not spend the whole of the winter in a continuous state of torpidity. A temperature of about fifty degrees is sufficient to arouse most of them from their winter sleep, although the additional stimulus of bright sunshine is necessary to restore the diurnal species to a state of real activity. They are often enticed from their winter quarters by mild weather in very early spring, only to be driven back again by late frosts and snows; but, as a rule, they bid a permanent farewell to their hiding-places about the end of March or the beginning of April.

One of these is the beautiful little harvest mouse, which measures not much more than four inches in length, including the tail of about two inches. It is of a reddish yellow colour above, and white beneath; and may often be seen in cornfields and rough pastures. Sometimes it will spend the winter in stacks of hay or straw, and is then kept sufficiently warm to remain active throughout the season, feeding on such seeds or grain as it can find. It does not usually construct its summer nest till the end of spring or early summer; and this nest is a wonderful structure—a globular mass of intertwined grass blades, usually suspended from stalks of corn, with the aperture so artfully concealed that it is by no means easily found. Should you succeed in finding one of these nests, take up a position from which you can watch the owners, if only to see the manner in which they climb the smooth straws, curling their little tails round the latter to increase their hold.

Strolling over meadows or rough pastures, and intently keeping your eyes on the ground, you are almost sure to make the acquaintance of the little shrew, also known as the shrew-mouse and the short-tailed field-mouse. But it is not a mouse, nor does it belong to the same order. The creatures we have previously

named belong to the group of animals known as rodents or gnawers, and are easily known by the few sharp, chisel-like teeth in the front of each jaw, separated by a considerable space from the grinding teeth at the back, as may be seen in the skull of a rabbit.

*The Skull of a Rabbit*

All these rodents live principally, if not entirely, on vegetable substances. But the shrew has pointed teeth, the front ones long and somewhat sickle-shaped; and it feeds entirely on an animal diet, consisting principally of insects, worms, slugs, and snails. It may easily be distinguished from field-mice by its long, pointed snout, and its short tail which is not so long as the body. Shrews live in holes in the ground; and at the present season are engaged in rearing their young. It is remarkable that dogs, cats, and other carnivorous animals which devour mice readily will not eat shrews. The reason is that shrews have a strong, repulsive scent which, although it preserves them from the attacks of some creatures, does not prevent them from being worried or tortured to death by cats and dogs.

*The Shrew*

Hedgehogs are also now at large after their winter sleep. They belong to the same order as the shrew; but, being larger and stronger, they attack larger game in addition to insects and worms, even feeding on lizards, snakes, mice, and young birds from the nest. Since hedgehogs are chiefly nocturnal in their habits the best time to look for them is the evening, just about sundown; but they often come out to feed during the brighter hours of the day.

*The Hedgehog Feeding*

Although the hedgehog can run fairly quickly, it will generally put itself on the defensive when surprised, curling up its body, with head, tail, and feet all tucked away out of sight, so that it becomes a ball with sharp spines radiating in every direction. Should you want to take it for future examination, roll it into a handkerchief spread on the ground, and pick it up by the corners of the latter. If kept in captivity it soon becomes very tame, will cease to curl itself into a ball when touched, and will feed from the hand.

*The Hedgehog on the Defensive*

As soon as the air is sufficiently mild to call many insects on the wing, bats are aroused from their winter sleep, and come out every evening to feed. They may be seen soon after sunset flitting through the air in search of their insect food, which they always catch on the wing. At the same time you may hear their piercing squeak, so high-pitched, by the way, that some human ears cannot perceive it; and also the crunching of beetles and other hard-skinned insects as they are crushed in the creatures' jaws.

Bats, of which there are many British species, are strange animals. They are not birds, but insectivorous mammals, bringing forth their young alive, and suckling them with their milk. Their bodies are covered with fur much like that of a mouse, and their wings consist of a very thin membrane extending between long, slender fingers, the sides of the body, and the tail.

If it is desired to examine a bat closely one can best be secured by searching in its hiding-place during the day. Church towers, barns, hollow trees, and dark spaces under the roofs of houses are favourite resorts; and here bats may be found hanging, head downwards, by their hooked hind claws, fast asleep. They may often be caught in an ordinary butterfly-net while in flight, but this method of capture not unfrequently leads to the breaking of the delicate wings.

*The Common Lizard*

Now let us wander beside a sunny bank on a bright day, or on the sunny slopes of ground partially covered with clumps of heather and furze, walking very slowly and cautiously with eyes on the ground. At times we hear a rustling sound as of a rapid retreat, and may just catch a glimpse of a lizard as it darts away to a safe cover. But, continuing our search, proceeding very slowly, we at last find one which is undecided as to the presence of actual danger, and remains perfectly still as we look at it, yet always on the alert and ready to scamper away at the slightest threatening movement.

These little creatures are true reptiles, recently aroused from their winter sleep. They are often confused with newts or efts, from which they are quite distinct. Lizards have a dry, scaly skin, and never live in water, while newts have a soft, moist skin like that of a frog, and, when young, live entirely in water, breathing by means of gills like a fish.

Should you desire to catch a lizard, you may do so by a very quick movement of the hand; but grasp it bodily, avoiding the long tail, for the creature has a way of rendering its tail very brittle, snapping it off by a sharp movement, and darting away, leaving the still wriggling tail in your grasp. The lizard will probably bite you, but its teeth, though sharp, are so small that they cannot penetrate the skin.

Lizards make very interesting pets. They soon become very tame, and adapt themselves well to captivity; but when procuring or making a case in which to keep them, remember that they are good climbers, and can easily ascend any perpendicular surface that is not quite smooth. They should be fed on insects, grubs, spiders, and small worms.

While searching in the haunts of the common lizard, you will probably meet with a creature that looks like a small snake, not much more than a foot in length, if so long, with a smooth body covered all over with tiny scales.

*The Blindworm*

This is the blind-worm or slow-worm, also recently emerged from its hibernating quarters. It is not a snake, but a lizard without legs. Its habits are somewhat similar to those of the common lizard, though it is not so rapid in its movements. Having no limbs, it has to glide along after the manner of a snake; but it has the notched tongue of a lizard, movable eyelids (snakes have none), and the same habit of snapping its tail when caught by that part. It feeds principally on slugs and earthworms; and, like the common lizard, lives well in captivity. It seldom attempts to bite its captor, and is in every way perfectly harmless.

Snakes, too, have just left their winter retreats, and may now be seen in their usual haunts in wild districts. There are only two species of British snakes, the ringed snake or grass snake, and the viper or adder. The former inhabits damp, grassy places, especially in the neighbourhood of woods and coppices; and the latter dry heaths and moors. Yet they do not strictly confine themselves to these respective habitats, and it is not at all uncommon to meet with both species in the same spot.

Every countryside rambler ought to know how to readily recognise these two reptiles; for while the grass snake is perfectly harmless, and becomes an interesting pet in confinement, the viper is venomous. Both

*The Grass Snake*

vary very much in their general colour, especially the viper; so that it is not always easy to recognise them at a distance without noting their characteristic markings. The grass snake is of a greyish-olive colour above, but often very dark; and greenish yellow beneath, checkered with a very variable amount of black. Behind the head, above, there are two yellow or orange spots that give the appearance of a ring or collar (hence the name "ringed snake"), behind which there are two rather large black spots. The upper surface of the body is marked with several rows of alternating black spots, but there is no continuous series of spots forming a line down the middle of the back.

The ground colour of the viper varies from a pale grey to a dark reddish brown, but it may always be known by the large lozenge-shaped spots which, joined together, form a continuous zigzag line down the middle of the back. Its head is broader, proportionately, than that of the ringed snake, and is flatter above; and on its upper side there is a conspicuous black V-shaped mark.

*The Viper*

Both these snakes cast their scales a few times every season, and the finding of a complete coat of one of them is sometimes the first intimation that one is intruding on its haunt.

Frogs and toads are perhaps the earliest of all hibernating creatures to bid a final farewell to their winter homes. The former especially quit their retreat so early that it is not at all uncommon to see them actually imprisoned in ice in the ponds to which they have returned to lay their eggs; and the eggs themselves are frequently held icebound in late February or early March.

In early spring almost every pond resounds with their song; and it is easy to distinguish between the croak of the frog and that of the toad, for the latter is decidedly musical compared with the former. The toad is shown to the right.

*The Toad*

Newts or efts do not appear quite so early, but even these may be seen in ponds and amongst damp grass very early in the season.

On any warm, sunny day our beautiful hibernating butterflies may be seen on the wing, the males employed principally in sucking nectar from the spring flowers, and the females in searching out the food-plants of their future progeny of caterpillars, and depositing their eggs thereon. These butterflies include some of the most beautiful of our British species, and the commonest of them are shown below.

*Spring Butterflies: The Copper (1), the Common Blue (2), the Large Skipper (3), and the Dingy Skipper (4)*

They emerged from the chrysalis the previous summer, and live till about the end of spring, so that they exist in the winged state for more than three-fourths of the year.

It must not be supposed, however, that all the butterflies seen in spring are hibernators, for many of them are early species of the present year, having spent the winter either as grubs or as chrysalides.

A number of moths also hibernate during the winter, but these are not so likely to attract the attention of the ordinary countryside rambler, for the majority of them do not fly till dusk; yet they, together with early non-hibernating species, enter houses through open windows in the evening, attracted by lights within. A few of these are shown below.

*Winter Moths: The Humming-Bird Moth (1), the Spring Usher and Female (2), the Early Moth (3), and the Small Eggar (4)*

*Winter Moths: The Pale Brindled Beauty (1), Dotted Border (2), Oak Beauty (3), and March Moth (4)*

On warm spring days we often observe solitary wasps, always of unusually large size. These are the queens, the only survivors of the numerous large colonies that pestered us so much the previous summer. If you watch them you will frequently notice that they are searching for a suitable hole in which to establish a nest. Each one (accidents excepted) is destined to be the mother of a large family; and each one destroyed in the spring means one wasp's nest less in the coming summer.

The females of many of our wild bees also hibernate during the winter, and may now be seen seeking desirable residences for their progeny, or, in some cases, even gathering material for the construction of a nest.

In addition to those mentioned, a host of creatures is roused from a winter sleep by the warmth of spring. We have not space even to name them, but the countryside rambler will be continually meeting with them early in the season.

## CHAPTER IV

# WAYSIDE AND HEDGEROW

 AYSIDE and hedgerow are now beginning to look freshly green again. The new growths of perennial herbs and the first leaves of numerous seedlings are bursting through the withered stems and leaves of last summer; and the brightness of the green is enhanced by contrast with the sombre background. Vivid tufts of green also appear on the brambles and shrubbage of wayside wastes, and the shrubs and creepers topping the hedgebanks are rapidly forming their new shoots.

Even in early spring we find that some of the wild flowers have already finished blooming. The "lambs'-tails" of the hazel bushes are dead or dying, and rapidly falling to the ground; but the little budlike clusters of fruiting flowers, although they bear only the withered remains

*Flowers of the Hazel*

30

of their crimson, pollen-catching filaments, will soon begin to swell as the nuts commence to develop within them.

The white blossoms of the sloe or blackthorn are also fast disappearing, their white petals falling like a shower of snow on the ground beneath.

The tall elm and the evergreen yew, which often break the monotony of the bushy hedgebank, have both completed their flowering season. Winged fruits are already beginning to appear on the tips of the branches of the former; and the pollen-flowers of the yew are now quite dead.

Yet some of the flowers that commenced to bloom before the spring season opened are now to be seen in their greatest profusion. Shady banks are thickly spotted with the bright yellow flowers of the lesser celandine raised only slightly above the glossy leaves.

*The Lesser Celandine*

Intimately mixed with these we often find the sweet violet, the primrose, the little white strawberry-leaved cinquefoil so often mistaken for the wild strawberry, and, a little later, with the scentless dog-violet.

This admixture of violet, yellow and white, with its background of various tints of green, not unfrequently

The Strawberry-Leaved
Cinquefoil

The Red
Dead-Nettle

further varied by the little purple, lipped flowers of the red dead-nettle, forms a very pleasing picture.

The Shepherd's Purse

Some of the above flowers also adorn the weedy wayside, in company with the tiny white clusters of the shepherd's purse and the small white stars of the chickweed, both of which are to be seen in bloom more or less all the year round.

Then, before April is over, new flowers appear while all the above are still in bloom. In the shade, at the foot of hedgebanks, the tall stalks of the garlic mustard or Jack-by-the-hedge ascend rapidly, with their clusters of little white, four-petalled flowers at the top.

Also emerging are the white umbels of the wild chervil with its beautiful, fernlike foliage; and the white dead-nettle with close clusters of rather large lipped flowers in the axils of the upper leaves.

*The Garlic Mustard*

*The White Dead-Nettle*

And on the banks themselves there now appear the little blue flowers of the creeping ground-ivy, in clusters of about six in the axils of the rounded leaves.

*The Ground Ivy*

*The Colt's-Foot*

And, in damp places, bloom the yellow flowers of the colt's-foot which look much like small dandelions, but they are supported on thicker stalks, and always bloom before the foliage appears.

New flowers are also to be seen by the wayside, including the mouse-ear chickweed that may be known by its small downy leaves placed in pairs, and its forked clusters of little starlike flowers; the pretty dove's-foot crane's-bill—a species of wild geranium, the leaves of which are deeply cut into several wedge-shaped parts, and whose small purplish flowers are arranged in pairs; also, in very dry places, the rich purple flowers of the spring vetch, placed singly, without stalks, in the axils of the compound leaves. The last named belongs to the pea-flower order, and a glance at one of the little blooms will

*The Mouse-Ear Chickweed*

show that it is much like the garden sweet-pea in form.

Before the spring season is at an end, the number of wild flowers in bloom has so greatly increased that it would be impossible to deal with them here; and if the reader is desirous to identify all he meets with, it will be necessary to consult a rather big volume dealing with our flora only.

*The Dove's-Foot Crane's-Bill*

During the month of April the most hardy of our wild birds will have finished their nest-building, and already have laid their eggs; but May is the best month in which to study nests and eggs, this being the time when the largest number of species is engaged in raising their broods.

While gathering flowers in hedgerows one is occasionally startled by the sudden flutter of a bird that hastily emerges from a hole or from amongst thick shrubbage almost close by. When this occurs it is fairly certain that we have disturbed a bird that was sitting on its nest, and a careful search will generally reveal the nest with its eggs or young.

Some sitting birds are rather shy, and will fly from their nests when any one is still some feet distant; but others will remain at rest until almost touched. In fact a few are such close sitters that, if the exact position of the nest be previously known, they may be approached, cautiously, to within a foot or so, and be watched for some time without the bird showing any signs of fear. We have even gently stroked the head of a sitting bird without in any way interfering with its parental duties.

Since sitting birds are so reluctant to leave their eggs, wayfarers may pass many nests without knowing of their existence; and a countryside rambler who desires to make a study of our nests and eggs must adopt some means of discovering their whereabouts.

As a rule, nests are very artfully concealed from view, so that there is but little hope of finding them unless we have observed the occupants fly from them. The easiest way to discover them is to walk slowly along the hedgebank or wayside, gently tapping the bushes and herbage with a stick. But even then you will not always succeed in finding a nest in a place from which a bird has flown; and it is sometimes necessary, in order to be sure of the exact situation, to conceal yourself some little distance away, and watch for the bird to come back. The best way to find a nest in a thick bush is to look upwards through the latter towards the sky, for the nest will be more easily seen against a light background.

For the purpose of identifying the nests and eggs, full notes should be made of the position of each nest, the materials of which it is constructed, and the size, form, colour, markings (if any), and number of the eggs. Armed with such particulars, it is generally easy to obtain the names of the birds to which they belong with the aid of a good book dealing with birds and their nests, or by referring to the preserved specimens in a natural history museum. Whenever possible you should also learn all you can about the parent birds, and for this you will find field glasses exceedingly useful.

Several of our common birds build their nests in hedges, wayside banks, and bushy roadsides; and here are brief descriptions of the nests and eggs you are most likely to find:—

*Thrush.* —The song-thrush generally builds in a bushy hedge, a thick holly-bush, ivy, or in the fork of a tree. The nest is made of thin twigs, grass and moss, and lined with mud or cow-dung with which is mingled some fragments of rotten wood. The eggs, four or five in number, are greenish blue, with small spots of very dark brown.

*Nest and Eggs of the Thrush*

*Blackbird.* —The nesting-places of this bird are similar to those of the thrush. The nest is constructed with stems, grass, and roots, plastered with mud inside, and lined with very thin grass. The eggs are from four to six in number, of a light greenish-blue colour, mottled irregularly with light brown.

*Hedge-sparrow.* —This bird is not really a sparrow, and its correct name is hedge-accentor; yet it is nearly always known by the former appellation. It builds its nest in a thick hedge, often choosing a close-set, thorny bush, using grass, roots, and moss, and finishing with a smooth lining of horsehair. The eggs are usually five in number, and are of a bright greenish-blue colour, with no markings of any kind.

*Robin.* —The nest of the robin is generally placed in a hole in a hedge or rough wall, a hollow tree-stump, or in a thick bush close to the ground. It is constructed of grass, moss, and dry leaves, and lined with horsehair, wool, or feathers. About six eggs are laid, of a light reddish colour, more or less clouded, and spotted with pale red.

*Wren.* —The common wren builds its nest in quite a variety of situations, among which may be mentioned holes in hedges, banks, walls, and trees; in ivy, thick bushes, or clumps of dense herbage; and close to the ground under brambles. The usual materials are moss, dead leaves, ferns, and dry grass, with a lining of fine moss, feathers, or hair. The nest is generally domed, with the entrance near the top. The eggs are white, with a few light red spots, and vary in number from four to eight.

*Yellow bunting.* —Although the yellow bunting or yellow-hammer generally builds in the furze bushes of heaths and moors, its nest may often be found amongst the thick herbage of hedgerows and wayside banks, or low in brambles or bushes at the top of a hedge. It is made of dry grass, roots and moss, lined with horsehair or fine grass, or both. The eggs are about five in number, of a very pale purplish colour, curiously veined and streaked with a dark reddish purple edged with greyish violet.

*Chaffinch.* —The nest of the chaffinch is a marvellously beautiful structure. It consists of lichens, moss, and fine grass thoroughly woven together with an admixture of cobwebs, and lined with hair, wool, and feathers; and is built in a shrub or tree, frequently in the fork of a branch. The eggs are of a light bluish colour, boldly blotched and spotted with purple-brown, and four or five in number.

*Greenfinch.* —Greenfinches generally build in a thick bush or small tree, or in the dense herbage on the top of a hedge. The nest is made with grass, roots, and moss, mixed with wool, and lined with horsehair and feathers. The eggs are about five in number, white, lightly speckled with reddish purple at the larger end.

*Bullfinch.* —The nest of the bullfinch is a very peculiar structure, consisting of a rough platform of woven twigs, with a depression in the middle formed of grass and roots and lined with feathers. It is usually built in an evergreen bush, such as yew or holly, or in a very thick hedge. The eggs are about five in number, greenish blue, with reddish brown blotches and dark purplish spots and streaks.

Another interesting feature of the hedgerow and the weedy wayside is the abundance of climbing plants which are ever struggling upwards to reach the free light and air. Some of these do not flower until late spring or early summer; but the best time to study their climbing habits is the period during which they are thrusting up their young shoots, for their growth is then very rapid, and we have the opportunity of seeing how young stems, at first erect and self-supporting, make their early attempts to secure a hold on their stronger comrades. This study, however, is of so much interest and importance that we must make it the subject of a separate chapter.

## CHAPTER V

# HOW PLANTS CLIMB

TROLLING by the hedgerows and over-grown waysides one cannot but notice the tangled masses of vegetation in which the plants are so intermixed that it is often difficult to determine their respective stems, leaves, and flowers. Everywhere climbing plants abound, some clinging to their surroundings by hooks or bristles, some twining their stems round those of their companions like a corkscrew, some throwing out little tendrils that are always ready to grasp any stem within their reach, and others weaving their lengthening shoots between the confused tangles above them.

Whatever be the means by which these plants climb, the object is always the same, namely, to obtain the light and air necessary for the development of their flowers; and the result, produced later in the season, is a glorious display of flowery screens and festoons, and sprays of blossom dangling from the topmost branches of shrubs.

Some climbing plants, including many that grow in our hedgerows and wayside banks, appear, at first sight, to have no special means of support, and yet they successfully raise their summits, in spite of their very weak stems, to a height of several feet. How is it done?

*The Hedge Bedstraw*

Look at the common white bedstraw of our hedges. The base of its stem is thin and weak, and yet its upper blooms reach a height of four or five feet. It thrusts itself upwards, weaving its stem among the herbage or shrubbage above it, always keeping its uppermost leaves upright and closely packed together so that it can easily pass through small spaces; and then, one by one, it spreads its whorled clusters of leaves horizontally to prevent itself from slipping backwards.

Another similar plant—the goosegrass—closely related to it, supports itself in the same way; but this one has the advantage of numerous little bristles, on leaves and stem, with their points directed backwards, so that they form tiny hooks by which the plant is securely suspended.

Most climbing plants, however, adopt a method of clinging that is obvious at a glance. Of these we will first note the twiners—those which coil their stems like a corkscrew round their chosen supports. They have always thin, weak stems, and yet, by means of their twining habit, they are capable of rising to considerable heights.

Each species of twiner has its own method of climbing, from which it never deviates. Some of them always turn to the right, like the hands of a clock, as do the hop, honeysuckle, and the climbing buckwheat; while the bindweeds invariably turn in an anticlockwise direction.

*Twining Stems of Honeysuckle*

*Twining Stems of
the Greater Bindweed*

Nor is it possible to compel a twining plant to change its habit in this respect. You may wind any one of them the wrong way round a stick, binding it securely as you proceed, but the growing tip will immediately begin to obey the instinct of the plant. Further, these plants never select a very thick object on which to climb, as if they knew that the thinner the support the more rapid is the upward progress. In fact they are quite incapable of twining their stems round very thick supports. It is of no use, for instance, to attempt to train hops on stakes much over three inches in diameter, for they are unable to encircle them.

Again, the motto of the twining climber is evidently "Excelsior!" for, on reaching a horizontal support, or one that makes only a small angle with the level, it will leave it at once, and search for an object that will lead it quickly above its surroundings.

As a rule the twining stems grow and turn very rapidly, and it is very interesting to make observations on this matter, as can easily be done by putting marks on the stakes of the climbers in the garden. The tip of the hop will make a complete revolution round its support in about two hours, during warm weather; and that of the convolvulus in an even shorter time.

*Stem of the Birch Strangled by Honeysuckle*

In copses and hedge-rows may often be seen remarkable deformities in the stems of trees, like the one shown to the left; and the cause is generally very evident, for in most cases it will be found that the stem of the honeysuckle is encircling the deformed object. The honeysuckle stem does not increase in length in parts where it has become woody in structure. Thus, if it is wound round a growing object, the latter, not being able to force the gripping coils outward as it increases in thickness, is naturally strangled, frequently even to death.

On the other hand, we sometimes meet with twining stems on objects thicker than the tips of the stems could possibly embrace; hence it is clear that the coils of the twiners, in these cases, were able to yield to the internal pressure of the growing support they clasped.

Now what happens if the seed of a twining climber germinates in a spot where there is no support of any kind for the growing plant? At first the young plant will stand erect; for, at this stage, the base can hold up the small weight above it. But, in a short time, the top-weight has so increased that the stem bends over, arching more and more until the tip, turning round and round in its vain attempts to find something it can hold, at last comes to the ground again. A fresh start is now made—another attempt to reach a suitable prop, with the same useless gyrations, until it is again compelled to come to earth. So the instinctive struggles of the plant to raise itself continue in vain, with the result that it becomes a feeble and sickly being, often perishing without being able to produce its flowers and fruit.

Sometimes, however, a twining climber produces several stems, and these, finding no support at hand, seem to realise the fact that "union is strength," and so wind round one another, forming a rope or cable which is often rigid enough to support them until one or

*Stems of the Honeysuckle
Twining Round One Another*

more of the revolving tips succeed in getting a hold.

Sometimes, too, a single winding stem, failing to find a stay, will twist itself into a spiral which, resting on the ground, serves to form a base to carry the revolving top as it searches for a suitable twig for its grip, just as a snake will lift itself on its coiled tail in order to elevate its head.

It is not often that a twining stem is in danger of slipping down on the object it grips with its numerous coils, but this is possible where the climber mounts a smooth, straight stem without branches. In order to prevent such slipping the twiner is sometimes provided with hooks or bristles to make its grip more secure. A remarkable instance is to be found in the hop, the stem of which is armed with little anvil-like hooks that cling to any object on which it climbs; and the hooks have such hard walls that they are not easily broken by the strain of any downward pull that may be exerted.

We have already hinted at the possibility of a twining plant failing to find anything on which to climb, and, in consequence, becoming stunted and sickly. To avoid such a calamity many climbers do not trust to one, or even to a few, clinging structures, but produce quite a large number of twining tendrils that are always ready to grip objects on all sides.

*The Common Vetch with Tendrils*

Sometimes these tendrils are altered leaves or leaflets, as we find in peas and vetches; sometimes they are altered branches, as in the climbing corydalis of our thickets; or modified flower stalks, as in the passion flower; while in the clematis the office is performed by the leaf stalks.

The tendril-bearing plants thrust out their feelers in all directions, as yet keeping them straight, or nearly so, in order that they may extend them as far as possible into space; but as soon as a tendril touches a stem or twig, the stimulus of the contact causes it to bend towards the surface touched; and the bending continues, in the same direction, until the tendril has made several revolutions round its support. Often, then, the base of the tendril—the part that had not reached far enough to help in the encircling movement—will itself contract into a more or less regular coil, thus pulling the plant bearing it towards the newly-found support.

The rapidity with which a tendril responds to the stimulus caused by contact is truly marvellous. Often the resulting bending commences in less than a minute, and seldom is it delayed more than a few minutes. Also the short time required to complete the several coils of its grip is equally marvellous.

Many tendrils are not satisfied by simply extending themselves to find a stem or twig on which to coil, but will turn themselves round and round to explore thoroughly the whole neighbourhood within reach; and this movement is frequently so rapid that the revolving tip of a tendril describes its circle in a much shorter time than the minute hand of a clock. In fact, it is frequently possible to see it move.

Further, if a tendril fails in all its attempts to obtain a hold, it often becomes stunted and shrivelled; while, on the other hand, if it succeeds, it becomes thicker

and stronger. Again, if a tendril which has recently coiled itself round a stem be gently removed from the latter, that tendril will gradually straighten itself again to make a search for another hold.

There is yet one other kind of clinging organ used by plants, namely, the climbing roots, of which we have an interesting example in

*Ivy Stems with Climbing Roots*

the ivy. Of course the ivy

has the ordinary roots by which it sucks up food from the soil; but the climbing roots mentioned are little rootlike structures provided solely for clinging, and have no power to absorb any kind of nutriment from the object to which they hold. How effectually they perform their work is shown by the tenacious way in which they bind their parent plant to the bark of the oak, or to the surface of a stone wall.

Brambles and briars are not always classed with climbing plants, but nevertheless they do very frequently climb when the opportunity presents itself. They thrust their fast-growing suckers and branches between the twigs of neighbouring shrubs, and then hold on by means of the numerous prickles with which both stems and leaf-ribs are provided;

*Hooked Prickles of the Wild Rose*

and as the points of the prickles are generally turned downwards, they form admirable hooks for suspension.

These prickles, by the way, are not needed solely for climbing purposes, but are also a valuable protection against the attacks of browsing animals.

When brambles and briars grow on moorland or other open ground, where they have not the chance to climb, their weak stems bend to the ground and form a series of arches in all directions, thus securing the abundance of light and air necessary for their robust growth and the development of their flowers and fruit.

## CHAPTER VI

# THE WOODS IN SPRING

 E have already observed the opening buds at the commencement of the season, and we now pay a visit to the woods a little later, when the trees are clothed with their first leaves. The tints of the foliage are now exceedingly delicate, the green being usually of a very pale shade, and often decidedly yellowish. Many of the leaves, though almost fully grown, still retain evidences of the manner in which they were folded in the bud, and some are still clothed with the soft silky hairs that were so necessary to them in their early stages. But the outer wall of the epidermis has now thickened slightly, so that the leaves are no longer in danger of being dried and withered by sun and wind; hence they have all spread themselves horizontally in order better to catch the rays of the warm sun.

As we walk among the lower branches of the trees we cannot but notice how artfully the leaves have arranged themselves to secure the maximum of light, avoiding that overlapping which would result in the shadows of

*A Twig of the Hazel*

some falling on others. In many instances where the leaves are rather closely set they have placed themselves so neatly edge to edge that they remind us of mosaic work. Often we see a small leaf just filling in a space where one of the normal size would cause some overshadowing; and where the leaf-stalks are nearly all directed forwards, towards the tip of the twig, we now and again notice one bent backward in order that its blade may just fit into an otherwise vacant space. Even the twigs which bear the leaves frequently take an active part in this scheme to catch as much light as possible, for they assume a zigzag course as they grow, with a moderately sharp bend at the junction of each leaf, thus keeping the leaf-blades more effectually spread for light and air.

*A Beech Twig*

The best examples of such leaf-mosaics are naturally to be found in just those places where the demand for light is most pressing—in narrow, shady woodland paths where much of the light is shut off by the upper, overhanging branches of tall trees; or on young trees which are overshadowed by larger ones. Some remarkable examples may also be seen where ivy covers the bole of an old oak, or in shady spots where this creeper trails over the ground. Here may often be seen the projecting angles of leaves just fitting nicely into the spaces between the lobes of their neighbours. Where the shade is deep, much overlapping is seldom found.

Many woodland paths are still covered with the decaying leaves of the previous summer, and even these leaves are worthy of a little notice, apart from the fact that their decayed remains help to produce a very rich soil. The soft, cellular tissue

*Skeleton Leaf of the Black Poplar*

of a leaf decays much more rapidly than the fibrous veins intersecting it; and at the present time we may see many old leaves in which the former has nearly or entirely disappeared while the latter are all intact. Such are called skeleton leaves, and they are interesting inasmuch as they often display the most delicate network of veins, the smallest of which are barely noticeable before decay sets in. The best examples of skeleton leaves are to be seen in wet places which are not much frequented.

Leaving the woodland path, and wandering among the taller forest trees, we may meet with hundreds of little seedling trees just peeping above the ground, often so thickly set that it is almost impossible to move without crushing some of them. But these seedlings, at present, bear not the slightest resemblance to their parent trees. They consist only of a little stem, with a tapering root below, and two small, smooth leaves and a tiny bud above. The two leaves are nothing like those of the parent tree. They were formed from two parts of the seed, and are known as seed-leaves. They originally contained a store of food material to support the young plant in its earlier stages; and after they rose above the soil they became green and were then able to manufacture a certain amount of material further to maintain the young plant. But these seed-leaves never live long. Other leaves arise from the little bud at the top—leaves which resemble those of the parent tree; and when these are large enough to manufacture the organic matter necessary for growth, the seed-leaves, having served their temporary purpose, wither and drop.

At first, then, it is not easy to identify the seedling trees; but as soon as the first foliage leaves appear the difficulty is removed. Of course it would be impossible for the numerous young trees to grow to any size, so thickly are they distributed; but they are exposed to so many dangers that but few survive the seedling stage.

A few of our wood-
land ferns remain green
throughout the year, but
before the spring is over
numerous new fronds
display their delicate
green—the bracken
in open spaces, and
other species on the
shady banks of tracks
and streamlets. And
note how these fronds
unfold, for the method
is the same in all ferns.
At first they are closely
coiled like the top of a

*Expanding Fronds*
*of the Male Fern*

bishop's crosier, and often protected by a dense, shaggy
covering of thin brown scales; then, as the fronds
lengthen, the coil gradually unfurls, exposing the
delicate green wings.

These early fronds are all produced from perennial
stocks which may have existed for many years, but
minute young ferns are to be seen at the same time.
The latter, however, would not be recognised as ferns
except by those who are acquainted with the life-history
of these peculiar plants. They are not produced from
seeds, like flowering plants and trees, but from minute
spores which are liberated from little cases on the backs
of the fronds, and carried as a fine dust by the breeze.

If a spore alights on a favourable spot, where there is sufficient warmth and moisture for its growth, it produces a little green, heart-shaped leaf or scale, with several minute rootlets passing from its under surface into the soil. This scale never grows large, but it bears little bodies which, when fertilised, give rise to the fern. Thus it will be seen that there are two distinct stages in the life-history of a fern.

As we pass beneath the overhanging branches of trees we observe a large number of caterpillars, of various forms, colours, and sizes, dangling at the ends of very fine silken threads. These are often so abundant in the spring that it is quite impossible to avoid them all, and we find ourselves soon encumbered with a number of them. Give one of the branches a sharp tap with a stick and many others fall from their resting-place, some reaching the ground, but always at the end of a newly-spun thread, and others only descending a few inches or feet. As soon as the threatened danger is over, they commence to return to their former places, and it is interesting to watch them climb the delicate thread, swinging the forepart of the body alternately to right and left as they grip afresh.

Millions of these caterpillars are devoured by birds, yet sufficient are often left to completely denude the trees on which they live. Oak trees in particular are seriously attacked by them, and it is not at all uncommon to see oaks that were densely covered with new foliage only a week or two since, now as bare as in the depths of winter. But the oak is a sturdy tree, and capable of withstanding attacks that would seriously injure or even kill other species; and in a few weeks, when the caterpillars have all changed to chrysalides or moths, we see a second crop of leaves making their appearance.

Sometimes it happens that most of the early foliage of an oak is devoured by these pests, but here and there some few twigs have escaped their ravages. Then, when the second crop of leaves appears, the effect is very peculiar; for the early leaves which were spared have now assumed the darker green summer tint that contrasts strangely with the pale green of the new leaves.

Although the caterpillars referred to are so destructive, yet they are really interesting creatures, and a little time may well be spent in watching their forms and habits. Some have sixteen walking appendages—six true legs just behind the head, and five pairs of soft legs, bearing little hooks, farther back—and these creep along with a wavelike movement.

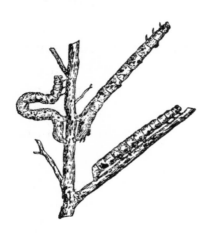

*Two Loopers*

Others have only two pairs of the soft legs or claspers, at the hindmost extremity of the body, and so they are compelled to progress by a series of strides, at each of which the body is drawn into a loop. They are commonly named the "loopers."

Many of the loopers afford remarkable examples of protective resemblance.

They are coloured with tints which closely match those of young twigs—various shades of green, grey, brown, etc.—and often bear marks and irregularities of surface resembling the variegations and notches of stems. They also have the habit of fixing themselves only by their claspers, when at rest, and of extending their bodies so that they are quite straight and form an angle with the stem corresponding with that of a young twig or leaf-stalk. In this position they will remain perfectly still for hours together; and their resemblance to the twigs of the trees on which they live is so true that you cannot always distinguish the former from the latter without a very close examination or a touch. Of course this resemblance to their surroundings is a great protection from birds and other insectivorous creatures.

*The Wood Anemone*

Some of the flowers of shady banks also flourish in woodland, especially among bushes and under-wood. Here we find violets and primroses mingled with the bright yellow daffodil and the graceful wood-anemone or wind-flower.

A little later, just when the daffodils are beginning to form their fruits, the wild hyacinth or bluebell appears, and the less conspicuous greenish flowers of the wood-spurge and the mercury.

*The Wood Spurge*          *The Dog's Mercury*

Later still, in May, we find the pretty yellow wood-pimpernel, the white wood-sorrel, and the wild strawberry.

*The Wood Pimpernel*          *The Wood Sorrel*

Of these the wood-sorrel is particularly interesting on account of the peculiar movements of its leaves. Each leaf is made up of three distinct, heart-shaped leaflets. As long as the plant is sheltered from sun and wind the leaflets are all spread horizontally; but when exposed to direct sunshine or a dry wind, the leaflets fold themselves closely to avoid unnecessary exposure, each one folding itself along the midrib like a sheet of paper, bringing together the two halves of the under surface, where are situated the little holes (*stomata*) through which moisture is chiefly lost.

*The Ramsons*

In damp places, where the alder, poplars, and willows thrive best, we may meet with the ramsons, easily known by its umbels of white, starlike flowers, and its strong odour of garlic.

Also quite a number of species of rushes and sedges, the former usually with cylindrical stems and clusters of small brown flowers; and the latter with grasslike leaves, and green flowers in close spikes. The flowers of rushes are perfect, each one having both stamens and seed-case or ovary; while in the sedges there are two distinct kinds of flowers, one kind bearing the stamens only, and the other the ovaries.

The most conspicuous of the woodland grasses, at this season, is the melic; in fact it is probably the only one to be seen in flower. It is really a beautiful grass, growing to a height of from one to two feet, with very slender stems and long, narrow leaves. In most grasses the little flowers are grouped together in spikelets, but in the wood-melic the blooms are larger than usual, and arranged singly.

During the spring season we have the opportunity of seeing many of our forest trees in flower; yet it is strange

*The Wood Melic Grass*

that so few countryside ramblers are acquainted with most of their blossoms. This is probably due to the

*Flowers of the Ash*

fact that many town-dwellers do not resort to the country much until the summer, and partly because a number of the tree-blooms are not very conspicuous.

At the commencement of spring the flowers of the yew, elm, hazel, and sloe are practically over, but in April the ash twigs bear their dense clusters of flowers, before the

61

*Catkins of the Birch*

*Flowers of the Oak*

leaves appear; the birch catkins have assumed their full size, the larger, drooping ones shedding their abundant pollen; and the beech, oak, and hornbeam blossoms are mingled with their early leaves.

But the most conspicuous tree-blossom of this month is undoubtedly that of the great sallow. As in

*Hornbeam*

*Flowers of the Great Sallow*

all the willows and poplars (the great sallow is really a species of willow) the pollen-bearing flowers and the fruiting flowers are on separate trees, and it is the former, in the case of the great sallow, that attract most attention, for the catkins are large, and of a bright golden yellow when the pollen-cases open. This is the bloom so commonly used for church decoration on Palm Sunday.

The flowers of many of our forest trees have their pollen scattered only by the wind; and, not requiring the aid of insects for this important work, they assume no attractive form or colour, and produce no nectar. It is otherwise, however, with sallows and willows. They need the aid of insects in the distribution of their pollen, so they bear rather conspicuous clusters of flowers, the more easily noticed because they usually appear before the foliage, and these flowers yield liberal supplies of nectar to entice their winged helpers. If you stand under a great sallow tree on a bright day in March or April, you will hear the confused hum and buzz of thousands of tiny wings; and, looking upward, you see crowds of insects—flies, bees, butterflies, etc.—hustling one another in their rush for sweets.

In the following month (May) other species of willow are in bloom; the maple and sycamore display their loose clusters of greenish flowers, the former erect, and the latter drooping; the sweet chestnut is decorated with its thousands of slender catkins, usually about six inches long; the wild cherry and the crab-apple are both crowded with lovely white blossoms, the latter often assuming a pinkish tint.

It is impossible for us to deal further with the attractions of the woods at this season; but we may just briefly mention a few of the birds that are most likely to fly across our path.

The interesting tits may be seen climbing over the branches of trees, often back downwards, searching for insects. Two of these—the great tit and the blue tit—together with the nuthatch, the woodpecker and tree-creeper, build their nests in holes in trees, and may be seen busily popping in and out as they feed their young. The nests are often in such small, dark holes that it is impossible to reach or see them.

Where you hear the familiar song of the ring-dove you may often be successful in finding its nest—a mere platform of twigs, with two white, glossy eggs lying *on*, not *in*, it. It seems surprising that the eggs do not roll off when the slender branches bearing the nest sway with the wind.

On the ground you may meet with the nest of the pheasant, a mere hollow in the soil, in which are laid about a dozen olive-brown eggs. The bird sits so closely on the nest, and is so difficult to distinguish on account of her inconspicuous dusky tints, that one might almost tread on the nest before she moves. The nest of the woodcock is similar, but is usually concealed among dead ferns or fallen leaves, and the eggs, which are very pale yellow, spotted and blotched at the larger end with grey and brown, number only four.

# CHAPTER VII

# FIELDS AND PASTURES

E do not meet with a great variety of spring flowers in well-kept meadows, but rough pastures and cultivated fields provide a number of interesting species.

During March hardly any flowers are to be seen except those which bloom more or less throughout the year and the loose clusters of the annual meadow grass. But in the following month several new flowers appear, including the familiar daisies and dandelions. These two flowers belong to the group known as "composites," each so-called flower being really a mass of small blooms densely packed on a common receptacle. In the daisy there are a number of minute perfect flowers forming a disc or centre, round which are the spreading rays of white imperfect blooms; but in the dandelion there is no division into disc and rays, all the flowers of the cluster being similar.

These two species are so common that they attract but little attention, yet only those who have taken the trouble to examine the individual florets with a

*The Butterbur*

magnifying lens can have any idea of their wonderful structure. They are further interesting on account of their regular periods of opening and closing—of awakening and going to sleep. Both require the aid of insects to transfer their pollen from flower to flower; and they open in the morning, when the particular insects they require are on the wing, closing again later in the day to prevent loss of pollen when those insects are also at rest.

In damp meadows we may meet with the butterbur, another composite flower, but very different in general appearance. Its flower-stalk is very thick, with many heads of dull purple flowers; and the plant is remarkable for the fact that the leaves do not appear until the flowers are nearly

*The Fox-Tail Grass*

over.

Another well-known grass—the foxtail—is also in bloom at this time.

During May immense changes take place in the general appearance of meadows and pastures. The grass is becoming rapidly taller, complete-ly hiding the withered blades of the previous summer, and wild flowers

*The Cuckoo Flower*

are thrusting their heads above it in great abundance. Each meadow seems to have its own favourite blossom; and, as we stand on some vantage ground from which we can cast an eye over hill and dale, we see one meadow yellow with the golden butter-cups or cowslips, another white with the daisy or the creeping clover, and a third bright red with the sorrel. Then, approaching each of these in turn, we find the general colour, as

*The Early Orchis*

viewed from a distance, is relieved by dots and patches of other tints—here patches of the purple clover, there

67

the pale lilac of the cuckoo-flower, and sometimes mingled with these the purple spikes of the early and the green-winged orchids.

*The Sweet Vernal Grass*

Most of the grasses do not flower till the haying time, but a few species are in bloom this month, one of which—the sweet vernal grass—we must note, because this is the grass chiefly concerned in imparting the delicious odour to new-mown hay.

The term "buttercup" is applied, and correctly so, to several different species of flowers. Three or four of these are quite common in meadows and pastures, and yet many countryside ramblers cannot distinguish between them. The first two to flower are the bulbous buttercup, best distinguished by the swollen, bulblike root, but also by the position of the sepals of the flower, which always turn down against the stalk as soon as the flower opens; and the small-flowered buttercup, which is not nearly so common. Then, about the end of spring, we get the tall meadow buttercup and the creeping buttercup. The former of these is much like the bulbous species, but is much taller, as a rule, and its sepals always remain extended when the flower is open; the latter may easily be known by its running

*The Cut-Leaved Crane's-Bill*　　　*The Dove's-Foot Crane's-Bill*

stems, which form new roots and new plants as they creep along the ground.

Cultivated fields yield a much greater variety of flowers than grass land, and before the spring is over the number of even common species in bloom is so large that we could not find space to describe them all. Nevertheless, every lover of Nature will find a keen delight in examining these flowers, some of which, though they may be small, are remarkably beautiful, particularly the pink crane's-bills, the bright-blue speedwells, and the scarlet pimpernel.

*The Scarlet Pimpernel*

As we wander through the grass in spring we often disturb the hen skylark as she sits on her nest. Searching the spot from which she rose we may find the nest, in spite of the fact that it is often artfully concealed beneath an arching tuft of grass. This nest is built in a slight hollow in the ground, and is formed of moss and grass, with a lining of hair and fine fibres. The eggs are of a dull pale green or yellowish brown, with purplish markings and reddish-brown spots, and are four or five in number.

The tree pipit or tree lark and the meadow pipit or titlark also build on the ground in meadows and pastures. The nest of the former is made of fine grass and roots, often with a little moss, and lined with hair. It is always situated near a hedge or tree on which the male bird spends much of his time. The eggs are about five in number, and are of a very pale yellowish or purplish colour, spotted and clouded nearly all over with shades of greyish brown and purple; but the ground colour and markings are both so variable that it is often difficult to identify the eggs without seeing the bird. The tree pipit is one of our summer visitors. It arrives here in April, and remains with us until September or October.

The meadow pipit is found more in rough pastures than in meadows, and its nest is often concealed under a tuft of heather or rough herbage. The eggs, about five in number, are very variable in colour, but are generally of a brownish white, mottled all over with a darker greyish brown.

Still another nest is commonly to be found on

the ground in pastures—that of the chiff-chaff, which generally builds on the weedy borders of fields or under the shelter of the hedges. In this case the nest is made of dead leaves, grass and moss, and lined with feathers; and it is domed, so that the opening is at the side.

We have already referred to the hibernating butterflies which leave their winter quarters permanently as soon as the days become bright and warm. These may be seen in abundance in fields and pastures, more especially round the flowery borders. In addition, some of the early species which have existed through the winter, either in the caterpillar or the chrysalis state, are now on the wing.

In April the white butterflies—the large white, the small white, and the green-veined white, all of which

*Spring Butterflies: The Large White (1), the Small White (2), the Green-Veined White (3), and the Orange-Tip (4)*

are responsible for considerable havoc in our vegetable gardens—appear almost everywhere; and the beautiful orange-tip butterfly, the female of which, by the way, has no orange patch on its forewings, is common in many places where the cuckoo-flower abounds, this being the food-plant of its grubs.

Other species are added to these in May, when we may see the beautiful little copper butterfly, the common blue (the female of which is brown) and the small heath, all flitting merrily among the meadow grasses and flowers. Also two of the "skipper" butterflies—the large skipper and the dingy skipper—belonging to a group so named because they never take long flights, but skip, as it were, from flower to flower.

*Spring Butterflies: The Copper (1), the Common Blue (2), the Large Skipper (3), and the Dingy Skipper (4)*

# SUMMER

## CHAPTER VIII

# THE WOODS IN SUMMER

OW comes the summer—the season in which both animal and plant life are at the highest flow. At its opening the trees are all in their densest foliage; wild flowers abound everywhere, more species being in bloom than at any other time; such multitudes of young birds have quitted their nests that the air is full of their chirpings, twitterings, and cawings; our wild quadrupeds have multiplied to such an extent that we are continually meeting with them or witnessing the results of their ravages; the air is so full of the hum, buzz, and flutter of myriads of insects we sometimes feel rather unkindly disposed to them; frogs and toads, which have been living their earlier days in ponds, now suddenly overrun moist meadows in such vast multitudes that they have led to the superstition that they fall to earth with the rain. While everywhere the eye and ear are impressed with the fullness of life, the air is filled with the sweet odours of a thousand blooms.

But as the beginning of summer betokens the

heyday of life, so the more advanced portion of the season brings with it the first touch of regret; for the signs of the coming fall begin to appear. The tall, waving grass, with its accompaniment of varied blossoms, has been cut close to the ground; and the ripening corn, with its glorious scarlet poppies, yellow marigolds, white mayweeds, and bluebottles, is nearly ready for the mowers. Thus we are reminded that the autumn, with its rapid decline of life, is near; and that the winter will soon be approaching.

But let us away to the shady woods while the hot sun is yet high in the heavens, and see what progress the trees have made since we saw them in the spring.

The forest trees are now in full foliage, and the tints of the leaves are darker than in the spring; for, under the influence of the stronger light, more of the green colouring matter has been formed; and even now we can see the buds, which are to lie dormant all through the next winter, in the axils of the leaves and at the tips of the twigs.

There is a great difference in the density of the foliage of different trees. Some cast such heavy shadows that hardly anything can grow beneath them; thus, in beech woods and pine woods the ground is quite bare except for its carpet of dead leaves or "needles." Others, like the birch and the ash, have a light, airy foliage that permits a considerable amount of direct sunlight to filter through.

Some trees which were in bloom early in the spring have already ripened and shed their fruits. This is the case with the elm and some of the poplars and willows. But many trees, including a few which bloom very early, form their fruits much more slowly, and do not ripen them till autumn. In fact, this is the case with the majority of the forest trees, and consequently this is a good time to watch the gradual swelling of the fruits while they are still green.

Yet the flowering of the trees is not all over, for at the commencement of the

*Flowers of the Elder*

summer may be seen the large clusters of white elder blossom; the yellowish-green flowers of the lime, each cluster of which is attached to a leafy "bract" that will remain to serve as a sail to aid in the scattering of the future seeds; also the two distinct kinds of flowers on the pines.

The flowering lime is one of the

*Flowers of the Lime*

midsummer glories that should not be missed. Resting in the grateful shade of a well-grown lime tree on a hot summer's day one finds the air charged with the delicious perfume of its inconspicuous flowers, while the abundant nectar provided by the blossoms seems to induce the companionship of all the bees and butterflies in the neighbourhood.

*Flowers of the Pine*

There are two distinct kinds of flowers on the pine trees. The fruiting flowers, which afterwards develop into woody cones, are in compact, almost globular masses, and, although now green, show a considerable resemblance to the future fruits. The pollen-bearing flowers are more conspicuous, for they are arranged in spikes at the tips of the twigs, and their pale-yellow pollen contrasts strongly with the dark-green leaves.

Another interesting feature of the woodland, especially underwood and thicket, in summer, is the abundance of flowering climbers, including the honeysuckle, bryony, woody nightshade, and the convolvulus or greater bindweed.

These climbers, however, are perhaps more at home in the hedgerow, and will be referred to in the next chapter. Then, as regards the woodland flowers of the low-growing herbs, these are so numerous that we cannot possibly deal with even all the common ones, but must necessarily confine our attention to a few species which are to be found in almost every wood.

*The Greater Bindweed*

Many of the spring flowers still continue to bloom. In early summer we still find the dog-violet, wood-sorrel, wild strawberry, wood-pimpernel, and wood-spurge; but these are now mingled with new species that have but recently opened.

Of the latter, few are more striking than the foxglove, the tall spikes of which often reach a height of four feet. The large flowers, shaped like a finger-stall, are usually purple without, and beautifully blotched and spotted within. Their pollen is distributed by large bees which enter the flowers for nectar; but while the insects are securing the sweets their hairy bodies brush off pollen which is afterwards carried to other blooms. The insides of the flowers are clothed with hairs at the mouth; and these hairs not only prevent pollen from falling out and being wasted, but also tend to prevent the entry of smaller insects which would remove nectar without in any way assisting in the fertilization of the flowers. The

*The Foxglove*

drooping of the flowers also prevents pollen from being washed out by rain.

Although not so striking as the majestic foxglove, the bugle makes a good show in the clearings of woods and coppices, where large patches of ground are often completely covered with its smooth leaves and rich blue flowers. The latter are lipped, like the flowers of dead-nettles; and the colour effect is increased by the purple tint of the leaves on the upper part of each spike.

In similar situations we may find immense clusters of the yellow cow-wheat, the flowers of which are in pairs and all turned one way. If you dig up one of these plants very carefully, together with the grass or other herbs

*The Bugle*

close to it, and gently remove the soil without disturbing the roots, you will find that a root or sucker of the cow-wheat is attached to the root of one of its neighbours; for the cow-wheat is a partial parasite which, instead of manufacturing all the material it requires in its own leaves, robs one of its neighbours of ready-made organic matter. Its own leaves do not appear to be

*The Tormentil*

*The Wood Sage*

large enough to supply its wants, so that it becomes necessary for it to steal in order to thrive.

In woodland paths we are sure to meet with the tormentil, easily known by its silky leaves, cut into three or five distinct leaflets, and its bright yellow four-petalled flowers, and also the wood-sage, whose inconspicuous, pale yellow flowers are very attractive

81

*The Wood Sanicle*

to bees and other insects.

More in the shade, among the trees, two other plants with inconspicuous flowers will be found—the wood-sanicle, bearing several rounded heads of small pinkish blooms; and the twayblade, a species of orchis with only two oval leaves and a tall spike of green flowers. As the summer advances there is a great increase in the number of composite flow-ers; these include several hawkweeds, some of which are very common in woods; in damp places several species of sedges are sure to be seen.

As a rule we expect to meet with butterflies principally in meadows and round the flowery borders of fields, but there are several summer species which fly almost exclusively in woods and coppices. The favourite haunts of butterflies are

*The Shrubby Hawkweed*

always those places in which the food-plants of their caterpillars grow, for the females invariably deposit their eggs on, or close to, the food of their offspring; and the food-plants of the species to which we refer are all woodland trees, shrubs, or herbs.

*Fritillary Butterflies*

These woodland butterflies belong principally to two distinct groups—the "fritillaries" and the "hair-streaks." The former are all very similar in general appearance, their wings being of a rich yellowish-brown colour above, with darker markings; and the under side is decorated with patches of bright, metallic silver, or with pearly white. Some of them are large butterflies, very powerful on the wing, and they frequently fly high over the tops of trees; but the females, especially, are often to be seen close to the ground, for most of the fritillaries lay their eggs on the leaves of violets.

The hairstreaks are small butterflies, very variously coloured, but easily distinguished from others by thin, white or pale streaks running across the wings on the under side. Their caterpillars feed on the leaves of woodland trees and shrubs.

## CHAPTER IX

# HEDGEROWS

EDGEROWS and wayside banks are now so full of interest that one could often spend hours in the investigation of a hundred yards or so, with a chance of finding something new at almost every step. The herbs have now reached their full size, and a very large number of them are in flower—tiny plants only an inch or two in height to tall herbs two or three feet high, with bold masses of bloom.

The climbers, for the time being, appear to be almost satisfied with their efforts to outreach their neighbours, and are now bringing forth their blossoms in abundance, some decorating the stems round which they have twined, and others bearing dangling clusters at their summits, or forming flowery festoons as their stems reach from tip to tip of the hedgerow shrubs.

Here is the favourite honeysuckle, its twining stems, always turning to the right as they climb, reaching the very tips of the hedgerow shrubs, where they produce dangling clusters of sweet-scented flowers which yield abundant nectar to the useful bees by day and to moths by night. If you examine these flowers you will sometimes find the tubes of the lipped corollas almost half filled with the sweet fluid which is secreted to encourage the insects that are so necessary to transfer the pollen from the projecting anthers of one flower to the equally prominent stigma of another.

*The Greater Bindweed*

Hard by we find the greater bindweed, the twining stems of which invariably turn to the left. Its very large, bell-shaped flowers are pure white, with a green, heart-shaped hood at the base. They are always produced singly, and are very conspicuous against the broad, triangular green leaves. Although this flower provides nectar, it emits no perfume to attract insects. In fact it does not appear to be visited much by insect life in the daytime, and it is probable that fertilization is effected chiefly during the night, at which time the white corolla would attract nocturnal insects from a considerable distance.

The woody nightshade is another very common hedgerow climber. This plant is often wrongly named the deadly nightshade, but the latter is of a very different nature. It is not a climber, but an erect, bushy herb, with purplish, bell-shaped flowers about an inch long.

The woody nightshade, on the other hand, is a climber, and its flowers are not campanulate. Although usually classed as a twiner, it supports itself among hedgerow shrubs more by interlacing its branches than by twining. Its leaves are heart-shaped, and often have two small lobes at the base. The blue flower at once reminds one of

*The Woody Nightshade*

the flower of the potato plant, for its five yellow anthers form a cone above the central seed-case, as in the latter. In fact the woody nightshade (also known as the bittersweet) is a very near relative of the potato.

In the southern counties the wild clematis or traveller's-joy is one of the most striking of the hedge-climbers. Its perennial stem is woody, and sometimes three inches in thickness, but the young branches are slender, and are supported by the leaf-stalks which twist themselves round the branches of hedgerow shrubs. Its loose clusters of flowers, though green, and therefore not conspicuous, are yet pretty; but the climber is rendered much more striking in autumn and winter by its white clusters of feathered fruits which have earned for the plant the name of "old man's beard."

Much more common is the black bryony—a climber that owes its elegance more to its glossy, heart-shaped

*The Black Bryony*

leaves than to its flowers, which are of a yellowish-green colour. This plant twines its stems on shrubs, and travels considerable distances over the tops of clipped hedges. It has two kinds of flowers—the male or pollen-bearing flowers, in long, slender racemes; and the fruiting flowers in much shorter clusters. It commences to flower before summer begins, and long before the end of this season it is laden with numerous berries, which turn scarlet when ripe.

The white bryony and the hop are two other common climbers which have imperfect flowers, but in both of these the male and the fruiting flowers are always on separate plants. The former clings by means of numerous tendrils. Its male flowers are pale yellow, and about half an inch in diameter; while the fruiting or female flowers are much smaller. The hop clings to surrounding shrubs by twining its stems, always to the right, like

*Male Flowers of the Hop*

the honeysuckle. The flowers of the male plant are of a yellowish green, arranged in loose clusters, while those of the female are in rather large globular heads.

Associated with the climbers above mentioned we are sure to see the beautiful pink or white flowers of the favourite dog-rose; and sometimes also its very near relative the sweet-briar, with rather smaller pink flowers, and foliage which emits an aromatic odour, especially when rubbed. The scent proceeds from numerous little glands which are situated on the under sides and edges of the leaves. These two roses are not usually classed as climbers, and yet they are, for they push their slender stems between the branches of hedgerow shrubs, and then support themselves by means of their numerous hooked prickles.

*The Sweet Briar*

Many of the lower hedgerow herbs are quite as interesting as the climbers, but we can refer only to a few of the more prominent of them. Let us first look at the two campions—the red or day campion and the white or evening campion. These two plants are very similar in their general form, but, as the names imply, one has red and the other white flowers. They also agree in that the flowers bearing the ovaries or seed-vessels

*The White Campion*          *The Red Campion*

and those producing the pollen are on separate plants, so that pollen has to be transferred from one plant to another before fertilization can take place.

The red campion flowers always open in the morning, and the pollen is carried from their stamens by day-flying insects; but the white campion always opens in the evening, and is pollinated by moths, which are on the wing at night. The flowers of the latter, being pure white, are easily seen at dusk, and they encourage moths by emitting a fragrant odour in the evening, and by providing nectar.

Nearly every hedgerow has its tangled masses of goosegrass or cleavers, the long weak stems of which, as well as the small, whorled leaves, are covered with hooked bristles to give support. At the tips of the stems are loose clusters of tiny greenish-white flowers, which are followed by little prickly fruits. Lower in the hedge you will probably find the avens, with its yellow flowers placed singly on long stalks.

Each flower produces a cluster of little fruits that terminate in a long slender hooked bristle, and both these and the fruits of the goosegrass cling so tenaciously that you will probably find them attached to your garments after you have been brushing by a hedge or walking by a weedy wayside.

*The Avens*

*The Yellow Toadflax*

We have space to refer to only two other prominent hedgerow flowers—the handsome yellow toadflax, remarkable for its lovely terminal cluster of flowers that remind one of the familiar snapdragon of our gardens; and the woundwort, with whorls of pretty, variegated, reddish-purple flowers, which protects itself from marauders by emitting a very disagreeable, putrid odour.

Passing a bank or hedge any time during the summer you see, here and there, a

91

hole through which wasps are hurriedly passing in and out. This hole is the entrance to the nest of a colony of wasps, often numbering many hundreds. You may stand quite close to watch their movements without any danger of being stung, provided you do not interfere with their work or their home. Those entering the nest are often laden with food for the grubs within, or with some chewed wood, worked into a pulp, for the repair or enlargement of the nest. Those leaving are usually without burdens; but sometimes you may see them bringing out little lumps of soil which have to be removed to enlarge the size of the cavity as the colony increases; and occasionally one laden with a deceased member of the community, for they never allow their dead to remain in the home.

*A Wasp's Nest (early stage) with One Side Removed*

The nest itself is a wonderful structure, and well

worth a close examination. To secure a complete nest it is best to destroy the insects, and that can be done easily by thrusting a suitable poison into the hole. Country chemists stock a "wasp destroyer," which is generally crushed or powdered potassium cyanide. Insert a dram or two of this substance through the entrance, and you will notice that while wasps are continually returning, none come out again. Allow an hour or two for the return of all the labourers, and then you may proceed to carefully remove the soil till the nest is completely exposed. It is necessary to await the return of all the wasps that were outside, otherwise the home-comers will attack you as you are busy with the excavation.

You will find that the nest is composed of a delicate grey paper, globular in form, and suspended from root-fibres that were exposed at the top of the cavity. Gently tear away the papery covering at one side, and you expose a home which may have several storeys, each storey consisting of a large number of inverted hexagonal cells. Some of the cells are still unfinished; some contain only a tiny egg; and others shelter white, legless grubs. A number of them are closed with a thin, white, papery membrane, and these contain fully-grown grubs which are gradually changing to perfect wasps. At the bottom of the cavity are a large number of dead wasps, including, perhaps, several females or queens whose duty is the laying of eggs.

It is remarkable that the poison which so quickly kills the winged insects acts comparatively slowly on the grubs, so that after the nest has been removed from its cavity all or most of the grubs are still alive; and if you transfer the nest to some sheltered spot where it can be observed conveniently, you will find, in the course of a few days, that some of the more advanced occupants have already developed into winged insects. A little later others will rapidly appear, and in turn the perfect insects take upon themselves the work of feeding the grubs and repairing the nest, so that the latter soon becomes once more a centre of life and activity.

The wasps' nest shown below was removed from a hedge-bank, and placed in a glass-fronted box, while still small. This nest was afterwards considerably enlarged, and eventually fastened to the sides and glass front of the box.

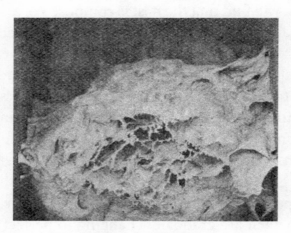

*A Wasps' Nest in a Glass-Fronted Box*

We have already mentioned the pretty lizards and blind-worms that inhabit sunny banks. These, of course, are to be seen all through the summer months, but now their haunts are enlivened by the presence of numerous young ones. Those of the common lizard are described in a later chapter. The young of the blind-worm are of a yellowish white above, and black beneath. When brought forth they are nearly two inches long.

## CHAPTER X

# WAYSIDES AND WASTES

ANY of our country roads have no hedges or banks, but are bordered by weedy strips of ground with, here and there, patches of waste land. Such roads are frequently separated from the adjacent wastes by a small ditch which is generally quite dry during the greater part of the summer, and overgrown with tall grasses and various kinds of coarse vegetation.

A number of wild flowers are particularly partial to such situations, including some which apparently delight in dry stony places with full exposure to the sun's rays; and so varied are the plant growths on these weedy roadsides that one may count scores of species without searching more than a few yards.

Here, quite within the range of busy traffic, and often smothered with dust in dry weather, we see the bright yellow flowers of the silverweed, so called on account of the white silky down which covers the under sides of its pretty leaves.

In company with this plant we generally find

chickweeds—the common chickweed and the hairy mouse-ear chickweed, both with small, white, starry flowers—but where the silverweed is well established other plants are usually crowded out, for the leaves of the latter closely cover the soil, and the plants spread rapidly by means of their creeping runners which send down roots and produce new growths above.

*The Silverweed*

Here, too, we find the scarlet pimpernel, and the broad-leaved and narrow-leaved plantains. The

*The Mouse-Ear Chickweed*

*The Scarlet Pimpernel*

*The Musk Thistle*

former is of very different appearance and habit to the latter, yet the fruits of both are remarkable for the manner in which they open. Most fruits which split when ripe open by longitudinal slits, but those of the plants just named split transversely round the middle, so that the top falls off as a little cap. The fruits of the plantains are very small, but the feature we refer to is easily seen with a lens. If the fruits are ripe a very little pressure will cause the cap to fly off.

Taking a general view of the summer wayside flowers one is struck by the abundance of composite species—those in which a number of little stalkless florets are crowded together on a common receptacle. The commonest of these to be seen at the present time include the yellow hawkweeds, the sow-thistle, various species of prickly or true thistles, the ragwort, chamomile, mayweeds and knap-weeds; some of these have two distinct sets of florets forming a central

*The Ragwort*

*The Wild Chamomile*    *The Knapweed*

disc and surrounding rays, like the common daisy, while others have only one kind, like the dandelion.

Where the ragwort and the groundsel abound one is almost sure to see beautiful "scarlet butterflies" taking low, short flights in the sunshine. These insects are not really butterflies, but are commonly regarded as such because they fly in the daytime. They are moths, called cinnabar moths. They may be approached quite closely when at rest, and then we see that the fore wings are black, with a scarlet bar and two spots of the same colour, while the hind wings are completely scarlet.

Towards the end of spring you may have noticed numbers of conspicuous caterpillars on the two plants referred to—caterpillars with bright-orange bodies boldly ringed with black. These are the grubs which change into cinnabar moths after a short period of rest in the chrysalis state.

We have so many insect-eating birds one may well be surprised that such conspicuous creatures as the cinnabar moths and their caterpillars are not summarily captured and devoured; but the very fact that they can display themselves with impunity is in itself a proof that they must have some means of defence. The truth is they have a very nasty taste, and that of the caterpillar appears to be more objectionable than the taste of the moth. An inexperienced young bird may once seize a caterpillar; but, if so, it will probably spend the remainder of the day in wiping its beak and in other ways endeavouring to get rid of the objectionable flavour; and certainly it will never touch an orange and black grub again. Moreover, the unfortunate experience will probably cause the bird to regard all brightly-coloured insects with suspicion.

Sometimes you will see the leaf of a thistle curled or bent and its edges bound together by means of silken threads so as to form a snug little tent, or two or three leaves drawn together for the same purpose and held in the same way. Open this shelter and you will probably find within a caterpillar which is black above and red beneath, with yellow longitudinal stripes. This is the caterpillar of one of our most beautiful butterflies—the painted lady; and if you would like to learn its future history, through the remainder of its growing stage, its quiescent state as a gold-spotted chrysalis, and finally its emergence as a painted lady, take it home, and give it a fresh thistle leaf every day, housing it in a ventilated box from which it cannot escape.

Wild geraniums are well represented on weedy waysides, and three or four species may often be found

*The Cut-Leaved Crane's-Bill*

*The Dove's-Foot Crane's-Bill*

within a few yards of each other. They vary somewhat in flowers and foliage. The former are always some shade of purple, and the latter more or less deeply cut; but all may be recognised by their fruits, which consist of five parts, united to a central axis in the form of a long beak. It is on account of this latter feature that the wild geraniums are often called cranes'-bills.

*The Shining Crane's-Bill*

You will also see several representatives of the group known as the umbel-bearing plants—plants whose flowers are on stalks which all radiate from one point on the main flower-stem, and are so arranged that they form a level or slightly

101

*The Hogweed*             *The Wild Carrot*

rounded cluster. The flowers of this group are generally white, greenish, or pale pink, and are never large. They include the fool's-parsley, cow-parsnip or hogweed, wild carrot, rough chervil, hedge parsley, and several others. The poisonous hemlock, also a member of this group, gives off a fœtid odour when crushed or bruised, and may be known by the purplish spots on its smooth stem.

A little farther removed from the stony line of traffic, where the soil is deeper and richer, and especially along the banks of wayside ditches, there springs a luxuriant growth of tall, coarse herbage. Here we find the goosefoot, with its dense clusters of small green flowers; some species of docks, bearing green flowers which often turn red, and which become sharply triangular as the fruits ripen; large patches of stinging nettle; and, especially in the ditches, a large number of grasses, some growing four or five feet high; also tufts of rushes and sedges.

Cattle are often allowed to graze by the wayside and on waste ground beside the roads; and in many places numerous rabbits feed on the same ground. In such spots it is interesting to note that while certain plants are cropped close, others remain untouched, and stand out in bold relief against the remains of the former.

*The White Goosefoot*

It is evident, therefore, that some plants are protected against the ravages of herbivorous creatures. The hemlock and some others are avoided on account of their poisonous nature, and also because of their nauseous taste or odour. The woundwort, though hardly to be described as a poisonous herb, is protected similarly by a putrid odour; and bracken and other ferns, the broad-leaved plantain, horsetails, rushes, and many other plants are neglected because of their objectionable taste, or on account of the large amount of hard and indigestible tissue they contain.

Roadside brambles and briars are protected by their sharp prickles, the hawthorn and sloe by their thorns, and thistles by the stiff spines projecting from the margins of their leaves.

Even some of the grasses remain untouched by grazing animals; and as you look over the ground where the latter have been feeding, you will notice large tufts of grass which were refused because of the stiffness and roughness of their blades and stems.

Again, not a few plants protect themselves by means of a covering of hairs, sometimes stiff and bristly, but often of a soft silky or woolly nature, and yet capable of causing much irritation to the mouths and throats of animals. A covering of hairs, whether bristly or soft, also protects plants from slugs and snails, for these creatures cannot creep over a surface so covered.

The stinging hairs of the nettles are perhaps the most wonderful of all protective structures, as far as British plants are concerned. Examine one of these hairs with a powerful lens, and you will observe that it is swollen at the base, where there is stored a small quantity of a powerful irritant poison. Then, strange as it may at

*Stinging Hairs of the Nettle (magnified)*

first appear, the tip of the hair is not sharp, but rather terminates in a little rounded swelling. But the latter readily breaks off when the tip of the hair is touched, exposing a very sharp edge which easily penetrates the skin, while at the same time a minute drop of poison passes through the tubular hair into the puncture.

Although the stinging nettle is so well provided with

multitudes of poisonous weapons, it is eagerly devoured by certain insects, and that with perfect impunity. Look at a patch of nettles, in a sunny situation, during July or August, and you will probably find scores, if not hundreds, of black caterpillars covered with rather large spines. These, when very young, live together under the protection of a common silky web; but as they grow older they gradually disperse themselves. If the caterpillars are black all over with the exception of their hindmost "legs," and minute white spots on the body, they are the grubs of the beautiful peacock butterfly; but if they are greyish beneath, and have two yellowish stripes down the back, they belong to the common tortoiseshell butterfly. In either case, take some of the caterpillars home, house them, and feed them daily on fresh nettle; and it will certainly be only a few weeks before you have had the opportunity of witnessing their wonderful changes, terminating finally in the emergence of really beautiful winged creatures.

It may be mentioned that the caterpillars described constitute the second brood of the year, for others preceded them in June, the first brood having been produced from eggs laid by butterflies which spent the winter in hibernation.

Other common butterflies are double-brooded, and on sunny waysides may now be seen the second broods of the white butterflies and of the beautiful little "copper."

# CHAPTER XI

# BY THE STREAM

EW countryside rambles are more enjoyable or more instructive than one along the banks of a stream, whether the latter be a swift mountain rivulet, wending its way among moss-capped boulders, or a silent, sluggish stream flowing through a broad expanse of meadow land.

On the banks we are sure to meet with some of the water-loving trees—the dark-hued alder, and various species of willows and poplars.

The alder is easily distinguished by its very broad, rounded, smooth leaves, which are sharply toothed at the edges; as well as by the ripening fruits which, at the present time, look much like small pine-cones.

There are many species of British willows, and it is not always an easy matter to distinguish between them without a careful examination of their flowers, which, in most cases, appear in early spring. However, it is not difficult to identify the commonest of the willows that grow on riverbanks, at the present season, by their general form and their foliage.

The largest of them is the white willow, which grows to a considerable height, and bears narrow leaves of an ashy grey or whitish colour. The purple willow has leaves of a similar form, but they are smooth and green above, and usually whitish beneath. Its twigs, like those of the white willow, are yellow, greenish, or purple, but it is a much smaller, shrubby tree. A third species—the osier—is shrubby, with long, twiggy branches which are used largely for basket-work and its long, narrow leaves are coated with a silvery down underneath. Then there is the sallow, a bushy tree with broad, wrinkled leaves, covered beneath with a short down, and of a greyish-green colour above.

You can always recognise a poplar by the peculiar way in which the leaves flutter in the breeze, swinging themselves rapidly from side to side with a rotatory movement. This feature is due to the fact that the leaf-stalk is flattened at the sides, and not from above, as is the case with leaves generally. Such tremulousness is most marked in the aspen, a rather small tree with rounded, deeply-toothed leaves that are very thin and pale, but not downy underneath. The white poplar is a much taller tree; and its leaves, which are larger and more deeply cut, are covered with a very dense cottony down underneath. A third species, the black poplar, has rhomboidal or triangular leaves without any down beneath. It is a tall, spreading tree, but a cultivated variety of it, known as the Lombardy poplar, assumes a narrow, pyramidal form.

Our ramble along the river bank soon convinces us that there are also numerous herbs which are distinctly partial to watery places, some living entirely submerged except, it may be, a few leaves floating on the surface; others standing in the water, but thrusting their leaves and flowers well into the air; and others, again, delighting in the perpetually moist soil of the banks above the water's level.

The truly aquatic plants—those which live exclusively in the water—are extremely interesting, especially when we study the various ways in which they are peculiarly adapted to their watery home.

The leaves of plants generally have numerous little holes in the epidermis or skin for the escape of moisture, serving, in fact, the same purpose as the minute pores in our own skin. These holes would be useless in the submerged parts of aquatic plants, and also on the lower surfaces of floating leaves which rest on the water; but to compensate for this they are particularly numerous on the upper sides of floating leaves. It has been estimated that more than ten millions of these tiny holes open on the upper surface of a single water-lily leaf.

Some aquatic plants do not send their roots down into the mud at the bed of the pond or stream in which they live, but merely thrust tiny rootlets a little way into the water to absorb dissolved mineral food. This is the case with the duckweeds, the little green fronds of which often completely cover patches of still water.

As the depth of the water is constantly changing with alternations of rain and drought, it is clear that those plants which are rooted at the bottom and have floating leaves must necessarily have some means of adjusting themselves to the rising and falling of the surface of the water. Such plants have very weak, flexible leaf-stalks or stems, which increase rapidly in length, if necessary, when the water rises, and bend easily as it falls again. In fact the leaf-stalks and stems are so weak that they are actually supported by the floating leaves at their tips.

Where the water is still or running sluggishly we are almost sure to see the large floating leaves of the broad pondweed, which sends its dense spikes of small flowers a few inches above the surface, and the floating, starry tufts of the upper leaves of the water-starwort that bears minute green flowers in the axils.

But few of the common aquatic plants make such a grand show as the pretty water-crowfoot. Its floating leaves, cut into three or six lobes, almost cover the surface of the water, and between them rise hundreds of slender stalks bearing as many white "buttercups." It has two distinct kinds of leaves—the floating leaves already mentioned, and submerged leaves which are cut into numerous very narrow segments in order that they may have more surface for the absorption of light; for the intensity of light is comparatively

*The Water Crowfoot*

feeble below the surface, and the plant must make an effort to obtain sufficient for its needs.

The Sweet Flag

In the shallower parts of the stream, particularly along the banks, we note a number of plants that have their roots in the bed, but display their leaves and flowers quite out of the water. These are commonly called semi-aquatic plants. Among them are the familiar water-cress, now tipped with a close cluster of tiny, four-petalled flowers, below which are little podlike fruits; the aromatic sweet-flag, with narrow, grasslike leaves two or three feet long, and a dense spike of little yellow-green flowers; the reedmace, often erroneously called the bullrush; and various sedges.

In addition to these we shall almost certainly find the water-plantain, easily recognised by its loose panicle of pretty pale-rose flowers; and the arrowhead, with large arrow-shaped leaves, and white flowers whorled on tall stalks.

The Reedmace

110

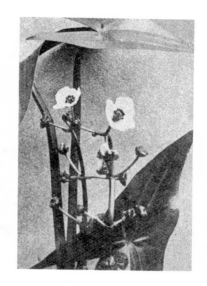

*The Water Plantain*

*The Arrowhead*

With the exception of the water-buttercup, the arrowhead, and the water-plantain, but few of the common plants living partially or entirely in water possess showy flowers; but those whose home is on the banks, just above the water's level, often display a blaze of gorgeous colour. Large patches of the bank, here and there, are covered with the bright-blue forget-me-not; while others are overgrown with the sweet-scented meadow-sweet, whose showy clusters of small yellowish flowers are often three feet above the ground, surmounting a pretty foliage of winged leaves.

Here, too, we see the lovely red-purple spikes of the loosestrife, two to three feet high; and the still taller great hairy willow-herb, with a profusion of rather large, reddish-purple flowers, each mounted on the summit of a long narrow ovary.

*The Great Willow-Herb* 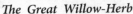 *The Reed Grass*

Numerous rushes also fringe the bank; and sometimes dense masses of the pretty reed-grass, which thrusts its leaves and flowers to a height of two or three feet. A variegated variety of the latter is frequently cultivated in flower-gardens, and is commonly known as ribbon-grass.

As we walk quietly along the river bank we hear a slight splash in the water; and, gazing in the direction of the sound, we perceive an animal, about the size of a rat, swimming rapidly through the water, and finally disappearing in a hole below or above the surface. This creature is the water-vole, but generally, though wrongly, called the water-rat. Its tail is much shorter than that of a rat, and although its feet are not webbed it is an expert swimmer. The fur covering its body throws off the water as do the feathers of a duck, and this feature causes the animal to glisten with a silvery surface when submerged. Unlike the rat, the water-vole is diurnal in its habits; and by remaining still near its haunts for a short time it is possible to see it fearlessly taking its meal of pondweeds or other vegetable matter within a few feet of you.

At this season the air over the stream and its banks is teeming with insect life—myriads of gnats, dragon-flies, may-flies, stone-flies, caddis-flies, small moths, etc., some flying singly as though searching for food or mates, but many collected in dense crowds and apparently enjoying a merry dance. Most of these insects have spent nearly the whole of their lives in the water, or in the mud at the bottom, as crawling or swimming grubs, and have recently changed to winged creatures to spend the small remnant of their existence in the air above.

Such transformations are really marvellous; and, if you would behold them, take a seat on the bank, at a place where insect life is abundant, and where rushes, sedges, or other semi-aquatic plants rise out of the water. Soon a six-legged grub is seen creeping up a stem or leaf until it is well above the surface of the stream, and then resting as if its journey were completed. Its skin splits along the back, just behind the head; and shortly, after a little wriggling and struggling, a creature with limp, crumpled, membranous wings creeps out, leaving its old coat, still attached to the stem or leaf, in such a perfect condition that it looks like a living thing. Even the slit along the back often closes so perfectly after the emergence of the insect that the rent is hardly perceptible. Soon the wings straighten and dry, becoming so rigid that the creature is ready for its first flight.

*A Dragon Fly*
*(just emerged from its pupa case)*

Some of the smaller grubs, including those of gnats, do not even leave the water, but simply rise to the surface and float; and the perfect insect, after casting its garment, actually stands on the surface film of the water to dry its wings.

The little moths we have referred to, known popularly as the china-mark moths, previously existed in the form of caterpillars which lived entirely in the water, protected in tiny tents constructed of the thin epidermis of the leaves of the aquatic plants on which they fed.

In addition to the winged insects previously mentioned, there are others which remain on or in the water, ascending into the air only occasionally, and more frequently in the night than in the daytime. Such are the little glistening whirligig beetles which run rapidly with a circular motion on the surface; and the long-legged water-gnats which dart about on the water in a series of straight lines. These creatures are so light that their feet do not break through the surface film of the water. Not only is the surface unbroken by their tread, but there is actually a slight depression where each foot rests, the surface film of the water being gently pressed down by the slight weight of the body.

Finally, other winged aquatic insects—various water-beetles and water-bugs—spend most of their time below the surface. But they cannot breathe under the water, and must necessarily come just to the surface occasionally, to renew their supply of air.

## CHAPTER XII

# OVER HEATH AND MOOR

NOW to the wild heath and moor, richly clad in a glorious mantle of purple, green, and gold.

Here trees are scarce, and those which exist are often more or less stunted and weather-beaten. A few solitary oaks stand out conspicuously in the midst of the moorland vegetation, proof against the furious blasts to which they have been fully exposed for many years; while the slender birches and other trees show unmistakable evidences of the ravages of gales they have encountered in the past, even indicating, by their permanent deviation from the perpendicular, the direction of the prevailing winds.

The foliage, too, is not so luxuriant as in the same species growing in fertile meadows and valleys. The leaves are smaller, and the shadows less dense.

But the glory of the moor and heath is due principally to the profusion of golden gorse, purple heather and heaths, and the seas of waving bracken—plants which are effectually protected against the attacks of herbivorous animals, the first by its spiny branches and leaves, the

116

second by its hard and wiry nature, and the last by an objectionable flavour.

The gorse, which blooms more or less throughout the year, is now full of flower, but the earlier blossoms, lower on the stems, are represented by their ripened pods which are incessantly bursting with a crackling sound and forcibly scattering their seeds.

There are two species of gorse or furze—the common one, which often reaches a height of five or six feet, and the dwarf species, with flowers of a deeper golden yellow, that is much smaller, and of a darker green.

Sometimes the dwarf furze is covered with delicate crimson threads bearing small globular clusters of red and white flowers. This is the lesser dodder, a parasitic plant which, except in its seedling stage, has no root in the soil; neither has it any leaves, and is therefore compelled to rob other plants of their nutritious sap. This same dodder also attacks heath and other shrubby plants.

*The Lesser Dodder on Dwarf Furze*

There are several species of heath and heather, with rose or purple flowers, but the commonest of these are the heather or ling, the

*The Heather or Ling*          *The Cross-Leaved Heath*

bell heath, the cross-leaved heath, and the fine-leaved heath. They are very attractive to bees and other insects, since they yield copious supplies of sweet nectar.

The open spaces between patches of heather, gorse, and bracken are particularly free from tall herbage. This is probably partly due to the fact that but few tall herbs could resist the sweeping winds of the exposed moorland and the constant attacks of herbivorous creatures. The flowering plants are mostly of low stature, and the grasses around them are generally cropped so closely that the ground is like a green velvet.

Nevertheless there are many exceedingly pretty moorland flowers, and these frequently appear in such profusion as to give a distinct colour to large patches of ground. The pretty harebell will be seen sheltering its delicate, drooping bells under tufts of furze, while in

118

*The Harebell*

*The Heath Bedstraw*

more open spaces there are dense masses of the little white heath bedstraw, the reddish sheep-sorrel, and the purple wild-thyme.

Then the grassy ground is dotted here and there with brilliant specks of colour—the yellow of the petty whin, a spiny plant with flowers much like those of the

*The Sheep's Sorrel*

*The Wild Thyme*

*The Petty Whin*        *The Milkwort*

broom; the small blooms of the milkwort, varying in colour from white to pink and bright blue; the pink or red clusters of the centaury; and the dark blue of the devil's-bit scabious.

We also meet with quite a number of composite flowers, several of them yellow, and somewhat like the dandelion, though much smaller—various species of

*The Centaury*        *The Devil's-Bit Scabious*

hawkweed and hawk's-beard. But perhaps the most interesting of these composites is the carline thistle, a very prickly plant, usually growing to a height of six or eight inches, with a head of florets about an inch in diameter. It is much like the everlasting flowers cultivated in gardens in that it does not readily decay when its flowering season is over, but looks much the same when dead as when alive.

*The Carline Thistle*

It is curious that the majority of butterflies which frequent heaths and moors are among the most sombre of the British species, their prevailing colours being shades of tawny brown, dull yellow, and grey; and thus they are not very conspicuous as they flit among the grasses and low-growing weeds. But in some cases the females are much more gaily decorated than the males, the difference being so considerable that the two sexes might be mistaken for distinct species. Nor are these moorland butterflies strong on the wing. They seldom fly far above the ground, and their flights are usually very short. Their caterpillars feed principally on grasses, and hibernate through the winter.

Heath and moor are the favourite haunts of the adder or viper, which has already been briefly described

*Moorland Butterflies: The Grayling (1), the Meadow Brown (2), the Large Heath (3), and the Small Heath (4)*

in an earlier chapter. Here, too, the common lizard abounds; and not unfrequently we see the blind-worm or slow-worm.

Rambling amongst the heather and furze you may often see the adder at rest, coiled up on a sunny slope, close beside a dense tuft of furze or heather which provides a safe cover in case of alarm. If you approach it gently it will generally remain quite still until you are within two or three feet of it; and you may remain observing it at that distance for some time provided you are quite still. But a threatening movement on your part will send it gliding rapidly under cover, with a hiss which may be intended either to warn or to terrify you.

Adders are much misunderstood by those who are not well acquainted with their habits. They will never attack a human being, even when threatened, as long as they have the opportunity to escape; but when at bay they will strike readily with their poison fangs.

When an adder is lazily basking in the sunshine, and especially after a recent meal, it is so careless regarding approaching danger that one might unwittingly step on it. This is dangerous; for, if the head is free, an attack directed just above the protecting boot or shoe may prove successful in producing two tiny punctures into which is injected a very powerful venom.

The haunts of lizards are very similar to those of the adders, and they will be found sunning themselves in little open spaces quite close, as a rule, to dense, bushy tufts.

Sometimes they will rush into their hiding-places before one has a chance to observe them, or even catch sight of them; but if one is walking slowly they will remain quite still, intently watching, until danger appears imminent.

During early summer there are numbers of tiny lizards of a glistening bronzy black colour. These are the young of the common lizard just referred to.

They are brought forth alive by the parent; or, rather, the young ones escape through the soft membranous covering of the eggs as soon as the latter are deposited; and they immediately commence to run about with surprising agility. The parent does not

*A Young Lizard*

123

appear to take the slightest notice of its offspring, and yet the young ones remain in the immediate neighbourhood of their mother's home for at least some weeks.

The blind-worm is not so frequently seen on moors, yet it is common where there is plenty of cover. It likes the sunshine, but not during the hottest hours of the day. In the morning it will travel in search of its meal of slugs, worms, and smooth caterpillars; and then retire under stones or in holes when the sun is high. It can climb almost as easily as a snake, and we have seen it basking in the morning sun on the top of a furze bush.

## CHAPTER XIII

# ROUND BOG AND MARSH

OST country ramblers are careful to avoid bogs and marshy ground, but those who stray even for a short distance into the water-sodden soil will find numerous interesting plants that are not to be seen elsewhere. Nor is it always necessary for one actually to enter a bog in order to investigate its vegetable treasures, especially after a moderate spell of dry weather in the summer; for the outskirts of the boggy area, while still sufficiently charged with water to maintain the usual vegetation, are yet firm enough to support cautious footsteps.

Marshes and bogs vary much in general appearance, the aspect being determined by the nature of the prevailing plants. Sometimes it is a mass of waving rushes and sedges, some species of which thrive only in soil that is saturated with water. Not unfrequently it is snowy white through the abundance of cotton-grass—a species of creeping sedge with triangular leaves, whose clusters of flowers form dense cottony tufts. At other

*The Cotton Grass*

times it is covered with coarse water-loving grasses through which peep the beautiful bright blooms of various marsh plants.

The heath or moorland bog is particularly interesting, and equally variable; sometimes it is almost uniformly covered with the whitish, cushion-like clumps of the bog moss, surrounded by a dense border of purple heather, and furze; but the pretty sundew may be so thickly interspersed with the moss as to give a decided ruddy hue to large areas.

It is curious that many of our common field and wayside flowers, including some which thrive best in dry, sunny places, have near relatives which can exist only in soils that are saturated with water. Thus the bedstraws of heaths and pastures are represented in the marsh by the white marsh bedstraw; the speedwells of waysides and waste places by the pale-blue or white

*The Marsh Pimpernel*

126

marsh speedwell; the scarlet pimpernel of dry waste places by the pale-pink bog pimpernel; and the wayside thistles by the marsh thistle.

Some of our bog and marsh plants are so remarkable for their structure and habits that they are well worthy of very careful observation.

As regards beauty of blossom, few can excel that of the buckbean or bogbean, which blooms just about the beginning of summer. The plant is a peculiar one. It has a creeping rootstock, with densely matted root fibres, creeping or floating stems, and leaves composed of three oval leaflets.

*The Bogbean*

The beautiful flowers have a white bell-shaped corolla, deeply cut into five lobes, tinged with red outside, and exquisitely fringed with white filaments within.

A few of our moderately common bog plants—the butterwort and the sundews—are especially interesting on account of their carnivorous habits. They attract and entrap insects and other small creatures, and then digest them and absorb the nutrient matter which they have thus prepared.

The butterwort will be recognised at once by the

*The Butterwort*

aid of the photograph to the left. It is a small plant, with a rosette of yellowish-green leaves close to the ground; and violet, lipped flowers placed singly on slender stalks. The flower has a rather sharp spur at the back, and the upper lip is covered with white, velvety hairs.

The margin of each leaf is turned slightly upward, so that the leaf forms a little shallow trough, the bottom of which is covered with a sticky liquid produced by numerous minute glands. It has been calculated that there are often as many as half a million of these little glands on the upper surfaces of the leaves of a single plant.

Midges and other small insects are attracted by the glistening secretion on the leaves, but as soon as they alight on it they are held fast, and every effort to escape only serves to glue them more securely to the sticky surface. Soon their bodies are completely covered with the viscid secretion, stopping their breathing holes and thus causing them to die of suffocation.

When an insect is thus entrapped, the upturned edges of the leaf gradually curl inwards, pushing the insect towards the centre of the leaf if it alighted on the edge, and in any case bringing a larger number of the

128

little glands close to it. But this curling movement is very slow, extending over a few hours.

The contact of the insect also acts as a stimulus to the glands, which now pour out an acid fluid that is capable of dissolving the digestible portions of the prey. In fact, the action of the fluid secreted is exactly similar to that of the digestive juices of the stomach of an animal. It dissolves all with the exception of what we may call the skeleton of the insect—the wings, claws, and the external skin;—and after about twenty-four hours the dissolved food has all been absorbed into the plant, leaving nothing but the indigestible fragments on the surface of the leaf, and the leaf expands again in readiness for the capture of another victim.

It is curious that indigestible substances, such as grains of sand, will cause a certain amount of movement in the leaf of the butterwort, but these will never stimulate the glands to exude the acid fluid which is necessary for the digestion of food. At the same time the butterwort does not confine itself exclusively to an animal diet, for its leaves will digest and absorb nourishing material from vegetable particles such as the spores of ferns and mosses, and pollen from flowers.

Equally interesting are the carnivorous habits of the sundews, which are often to be seen in company with the butterwort. There are three species of sundew—the common or round-leaved sundew, with leaves from a quarter to a third of an inch in diameter; the oblong-leaved sundew, whose leaves are about three times as long as broad; and the English sundew, the leaves of

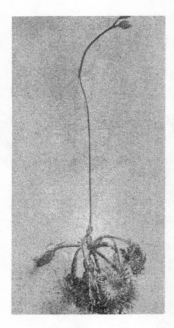

*The Round-Leaved
Sundew*

which are often nearly an inch long and about one-fifth as wide. The first is very abundant in bogs, the second moderately common, and the third rare except in some bogs of Scotland and Ireland. The habits of all three are very similar, and the following remarks apply to the three species.

Each leaf has a number of bright-red filaments on its upper surface and margin, sometimes more than a hundred in number; and as the filaments have swollen glands at their tips, they look much like as many minute pins. The under surface is smooth, and lies close on the ground.

The glands secrete a clear, thick, sticky liquid, which glistens like dewdrops in the sunshine, and is very attractive to insects. When a small insect alights on the leaf, it is at once securely trapped, and, as it struggles for freedom, its wings, legs, and body come in contact with the sticky globules of adjacent glands, till at last it is covered with the fluid and suffocated.

Now the leaf is stimulated to activity. Its glands become more active, and discharge a digestive fluid that is capable of dissolving all the nourishing tissues of the captive, and the filaments all round converge towards the insect in order to bring as many glands as possible around it.

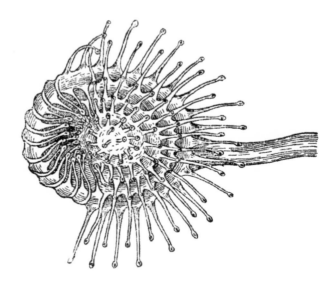

*A Leaf of the Sundew (enlarged) with its filaments converging over a captured insect*

These movements are much more rapid than the curling of the leaf of the butterwort; so rapid, indeed, that an insect is covered with converging glands in half an hour or less.

Sometimes it happens that two or more little insects alight on one leaf at about the same time; and under such a condition the surrounding glands will bend towards the nearest victim, producing as many converging groups. And if an insect is caught on the edge of the leaf, the marginal filaments will carry it inwards so that it can be reached by the largest possible number of glands.

After a day or two the process of digestion is over, and the filaments again extend themselves to attract and ensnare fresh victims; while nothing remains of the former meal with the exception of some dry, undigested parts which are soon blown away.

To observe closely the wonderful carnivorous habits of the butterwort and sundew, remove some plants, together with a little of the soil in which they are growing, transfer them to a saucer or shallow dish, and keep them very wet. They may then be fed on midges or other very small creatures, or even on minute pieces of raw meat.

In marshy ground of low level frogs are usually very abundant; here too the ringed snake hunts for its prey. But round the moorland bogs which are fringed with heath and heather the common lizard and the viper abound. Vipers do not enter the water so frequently as the ringed snake, but they may often be found basking in the hot sunshine under a tuft of heather quite close to the edge of a wet bog. In places where rank grasses surround boggy ground the lizards will jump, or even swim, from one clump to another in search of food, apparently attracted by the numerous spiders and insects which frequent such ground.

# CHAPTER XIV

# FIELDS AND MEADOWS

HE well-kept meadow is not particularly attractive to the lover of nature during the summer. If used as a pasturage for sheep or cattle, the flowering plants are cropped close to the ground, and but few of them are allowed to bear any blossom. Even the grasses cannot bloom, for their flowering stems are devoured as fast as they thrust themselves above the surrounding blades.

Nevertheless, we often find, here and there, prominent tufts of luxuriant vegetation that have escaped the ravages of the grazers, and which stand out all the more boldly when the surrounding grasses have been cropped short. These tufts consist of herbs which are disliked by the cattle either on account of their rough, coarse nature, or of an objectionable taste or odour. They include stiff grasses with rough blades, prickly or spiny plants, and various brightly-flowered herbs such as the ragwort and the woundwort. Wherever such rejected herbage is seen in pasture land, it is interesting to examine it in order to discover the means by which the plants protect themselves from attack.

*The Field Sorrel*

Many meadows that were reserved for hay presented a charming appearance in May and early June, when the red sorrel, yellow buttercups, white ox-eye daisies, and many other flowers were so numerous as to almost completely hide the grass. But all these were cut down in their prime by the mowing machine, and now but little blossom is to be seen except where the former plants attempt to produce a second crop of flowers and seeds to perpetuate their species.

Pastures which have been more or less neglected, both by man and beast, are much more productive of wild flowers. In these the red and white clovers, mingled with the yellow medick and hop trefoil, the pretty blue speedwells and field forget-me-nots, and the white-rayed daisies make a grand show close

*The Germander Speedwell*

134

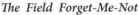
*The Field Forget-Me-Not*          *The Field Scabious*

to the ground; while above them mount the blue field scabious and chicory, the yellow hawkweeds and hawk's-beards, and the beautiful ox-eye daisy.

Many species of grasses are also now in bloom; and although their flowers are small and inconspicuous individually, yet the grace-ful spikes and panicles are exceedingly pretty as they sway with the breeze, especially when the dang-ling stamens are ready to yield the powdery pollen.

Insects are seldom seen on the flowers of grasses, for the latter provide no sweets.

*The Chicory*

They depend on the wind for the distribution of their

135

fertilizing dust; and for that reason not only are the pollen-cases well exposed to the breeze, but also the feathery stigmas, which are admirably adapted for entrapping the floating grains.

But most of the showy flowers require the aid of insects for the transfer of their pollen; and it is for this reason that they are attractively coloured, and also provide nectar. Wherever they exist, insects of various kinds hurry from blossom to blossom, each one, generally, for the time being, giving its attention to one particular species. Among these insects are many brightly-clothed butterflies, especially the little "blues," the burnished "copper," and the tawny small heath butterfly, their tints enhancing the glorious display of colour.

But cultivated fields, and more especially cornfields, are charming hunting-grounds for the naturalist. Such fields, having been left quite undisturbed for many months, are usually surrounded by a rich border of flowering herbs and hedgerow plants, while the fields themselves are decorated with numerous blossoms which, though a great annoyance to the farmer, are a delight to the country rambler.

The flowers of the border are frequently very dissimilar to those of the enclosed cultivated land; among them are numerous species of composite flowers, and quite a number of umbel-bearing species similar to the wild carrot and the hogweed; but a great deal will depend on the nature of the soil, for while some plants will thrive in almost any soil or situation, others are much more exclusive in their habitats.

It is remarkable that the flowers seen are often escapes from cultivation, and frequently mark localities in which they were formerly sown. Thus one may see crimson clover, lucerne, radish, turnip, mustard, flax, etc., growing wild in places where they are no longer grown as crops. And the charlock or wild mustard, probably introduced into Britain from Southern Europe, is so persistent in its appearance that it is one of the most abundant and troublesome weeds of cultivated ground, often completely covering entire fields with its golden blossoms.

Few fields are more attractive in summer than the corn-fields. Where the stalks are short, lovely flowers peep just above the ripening ears—bright red poppies and corn-cockles, golden corn-marigolds and charlock, blue corn-flowers or bluebottles, white

*The Field Poppy*          *The Corn Marigold*

*The Bluebottle*        *The Bladder Campion*

bladder campions, and white-rayed, yellow-centred mayweeds and chamomiles. But where the straws are longer, and these flowers are unable to keep pace with their growth, we see the latter between the cornstalks, making every endeavour to secure their share of light and air.

From the edge of the field we also note many lower plants which are content to bloom in the half shade of the standing corn. Among these are the pretty heart's-ease, several species of wild geraniums, white-starred chickweeds, the corn-mint, and yellow-green spurges.

*The Corn Mint*

Here, too, is the pretty but troublesome pink bindweed or bell-bind, which, failing to find a support, will trail along the ground. In the corn-field, however, the bind-weed is almost sure to reach a neighbouring straw, round which it will quickly twine its slender stem, and climb to a height of two or three feet.

*The Dwarf Spurge*

It is not at all uncommon to see ears of grain covered with a black dusty powder. This appearance is due to a fungus, called "smut," which destroys the grain. It is sometimes so abundant that a large proportion of the crop is lost.

Many of our wild flowers are so beautiful, it seems strange that, apart from some "improved" cultivated varieties, they are not considered worthy of a place in our flower gardens. It is true some of them are so persistent and dominating that, once planted, they rapidly extend beyond their allotted ground, and are not easily kept within bounds. But even though this feature may sometimes be urged as an objection to their introduction into our garden beds, yet it is very instructive from one point of view, for it gives us an opportunity of studying the means by which certain plants are enabled to succeed in the great struggle for life at the expense of those which are not so well equipped.

Few garden beds of wild flowers have a more pleasing appearance than one which imitates the flowery corn-field. Obtain some wheat, rye, oats, and barley; mix them, and sow the mixture in drills in a prepared bed early in spring. Then scatter the same ground with a mixture of the seeds of wild poppies, corn-flowers, corn-marigolds, chamomile, corn-cockle, bladder campion, and of as many other corn-field weeds as have been collected during the previous summer, and rake them all lightly into the ground or cover them with a thin layer of sifted soil. In this way a town dweller can produce a charming bed to remind him of the beautiful corn-fields which, perchance, he may seldom be able to see.

If sparrows witness the above operations, they will certainly pay a visit to the bed soon after you retire, and help themselves to a large number of your seeds. On the outskirts of towns, too, you may also expect field-mice to burrow along your covered drills, and carry off much of the sown grain. But you may considerably reduce such loss by moistening the corn with "paraffin" before sowing.

# AUTUMN

# CHAPTER XV

# IN THE WOODS

VEN in early autumn the woods and thickets are usually more or less sodden by the heavy rains of late summer and the copious dews of the chilly, lengthening nights; but all is, as yet, green and fresh save where the bracken displays its golden glory, and where the tall herbs that bloomed early in the year, and have completed the scattering of their seeds, are now rendered conspicuous only by their brown leaves supported on withering stems.

A few flowers may still be seen along the open tracks. As we pass, with springy tread, over the soft turf so closely cropped by hungry rabbits, we can hardly avoid crushing the pretty little tormentil, whose four-petalled flowers

*The Tormentil*

143

form bright yellow spots on the carpet of green.

Where the track has been sheltered from the more powerful rays of the summer sun, the turf is replaced by an equally soft and springy carpet of mosses, some of which are even now in fruit, bearing tiny capsules

"Like fairy urns on stalks of golden sheen";

and then, when the track winds among the evergreen pines, in the dark shade of whose heavy foliage scarcely a herb will thrive, the barren ground is thickly strewn with brown "needles" and old cones, many of the latter having been pulled to pieces by the busy squirrel to obtain the seeds that were concealed between the woody scales.

Emerging again into the open, where the track,

*Autumn Flowers: Wood Betony (left), Angelica, and Black Knapweed (right)*

bordered by underwood and shrubs, is not completely deprived of the warmth and light of the sun, we still find some wild flowers in bloom, most of which are not really to be regarded as autumn flowers, but rather as lingering blossoms of the previous season.

Among these are the tall wild angelica, with its broad umbels of white flowers; the purple-rayed black knapweed or

144

"hard-head"; and the purple wood-betony.

Along the grassy borders of the track, reached by the sun, grows the purple-blue devil's-bit scabious; and beyond it, more in the shade, the bright yellow golden-rod; while, suspended above, the last lingering blossoms of the bramble are to be seen.

*Autumn Flowers: Golden Rod (left), Bramble, and Devil's-Bit (right)*

And on the banks, where the track lies below the general surrounding level, the lovely ferns are still green; and the yellowish white flowers of the wood-sage still entice the wild bees to their liberal stores of nectar on warm, sunny days.

In the gentle hollow, where our path runs through marshy ground, we tread through dense clusters of rushes, whose cylindrical leaves remain green, though beaten down by the recent storms, and whose

*Rushes in Fruit*

*Autumn Flowers: Marsh Ragwort (left), Biting Persicaria, and Wood Sage (right)*

clusters of small brown flowers are now in fruit.

It is here, too, that we find the marsh ragwort, the biting persicaria; also the water-loving trees—the willows, poplars, and the alder.

The woodland footpath or open track is traversed here and there by little ridges of soil that have been loosened and pushed from below, a little above the general surface. This is the work of the velvety mole that forces its way through the soil in search of the worms and insects on which it lives. It constructs its subterranean run with remarkable rapidity, and it is interesting to watch the upheaval of the surface soil as the work proceeds.

*The Mole*

146

Where the hazel bushes grow, or where the beech trees have shed their ripe triangular nuts, we may see the lively little squirrel busy in the preparation of its winter stores. It is generally supposed that the squirrel collects all its winter food together in one secret hiding-place; but watch it from an adjacent cover, and you will see that it secures the nuts, one by one, and buries them separately just beneath the surface of the ground around its haunt. Many of these nuts are either forgotten or are in excess of the winter's requirements, and that will account for the numerous seedling trees that sprout up in the neighbourhood of the squirrel's home during the following spring.

Insect life is rapidly on the wane as autumn advances, and yet, on mild, sunny days, we meet with many species, even towards the end of the season, during our woodland walks. In the open spaces butterflies may still be seen on the wing, but these will be the species that hibernate throughout the cold season in the perfect or winged state, appearing in considerable numbers when called from their hiding-places in the following spring, by the warm sunshine, to renew their feasts of nectar from the early flowers, and to deposit the eggs that give rise to the next brood. They include some of our most beautiful butterflies, among them being the tortoiseshell butterfly, the red admiral, the peacock, the comma butterfly, the brimstone butterfly, and the painted lady.

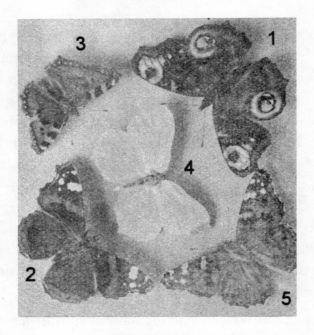

*Hibernating Butterflies: Peacock (1), Red Admiral (2),
Tortoise-Shell (3), Brimstone (4), Painted Lady (5)*

Wild bees are also at large during sunny days, searching for the meagre supplies of nectar afforded by the few late flowers; and in the damp and marshy spots dense clusters of gnats enjoy their merry dance in the rays of the setting sun.

But perhaps most interesting of all, as far as insect life is concerned, is the varied assemblage of winged life clustered round the ivy blossoms in October and November.

Passing under an ivy-clad oak on a sunny day, our attention is drawn to a continuous buzzing sound overhead, and, looking upward, we see numerous flies, bees, beetles, and butterflies hustling one another in their rush for the copious sweets provided by the globular clusters of pale-green flowers. This continues until the sun is getting low; and, at dusk, the late moths, nocturnal beetles, and other creeping things come for their share of the repast.

*Flowers of the Ivy*

On the borders of woods, among the underwood, and in the thickets, the foliage is relieved by the conspicuous colours of the fruits of shrubs and climbers—the black, clustered

*Autumn Fruits: Woody Nightshade (left), Hazel, and Black Bryony (right)*

berries of the privet, the buckthorn, and the so-called berries of the bramble; the bright-red fruits of the mountain ash, holly, hawthorn, wild rose, honeysuckle, woody nightshade, guelder rose and black bryony, and, close to the ground, the dense, showy clusters of the berries of the cuckoo-pint or wild arum.

149

*Autumn Fruits (from left to right): Guelder Rose, Wild Rose, Hawthorn*

As to the forest trees themselves, some of them have already shed their fruit before the autumn commences, and most of the others drop their fruits early in the season. Many of the hazel nuts have fallen from their leafy cups, or have been removed by squirrels, rats, and mice; the acorns, chestnuts, and beech-nuts are falling fast; the winged fruits of the ash, sycamore, and hornbeam are carried away by every breeze; and the old cones of pines and firs yield sooner or later to the storms. Several of these autumn fruits are represented here.

Some trees are particularly interesting at the commencement of the present season, inasmuch as they already display the flower-clusters which are to bloom in the following year. While the hazel still bears its leaves and its fruits, we see not only the so-called leaf-buds,

*Autumn Fruits (from left to right): Larch, Elder, Bramble*

*Autumn Fruits (from left to right): Oak, Medlar, Sloe*

*Autumn Fruits (from left to right): Holly, Crab Apple, Ash*

which are to produce the new branches in the following spring, but also the catkins of pollen-bearing flowers

*Autumn Fruits (from left to right): Sycamore, Honeysuckle, Yew*

*Autumn Fruits (from left to right): Pine, Chestnut, Buckthorn*

*Twigs of the Hazel (left), Alder and Birch (right), in autumn*

that are not in full bloom till next March. Although the latter are much smaller than the future drooping "lambs'-tails," yet an examination with the aid of a microscope will reveal all the parts of the flowers, even to the pollen grains within the anthers. Then, in addition to leaves and "leaf-buds," we find, on the alder, the larger catkins of pollen-bearing flowers, the smaller clusters of fruiting flowers, together with the old "cones" of the past season; and, on the birch, the old catkins which have not yet shed their tiny winged fruits, as well as the pollen-producing catkins that are not in full bloom till April or May of next year.

Later in the autumn the animal life of the woods has reached its lowest ebb. True the birds are always with us, for they do not hibernate, nor do they collect winter stores; and since the natural food of most of them is not plentiful during the cold season, they must necessarily be exceedingly active to secure sufficient for their wants. Many are occupied in searching for berries and other fruits that are left on the shrubs and herbs or have fallen to the ground, while the remainder subsist chiefly or exclusively on worms, grubs, and other creatures of the soil.

Insect life is now at its minimum, and it is only on exceptionally mild and sunny days that there is much on the wing; but the activity of the mole is always in evidence, and the scuttling of the surprised rabbit and the rustle of weasel and stoat in search of their prey are familiar woodland sounds.

At the commencement of this chapter we spoke of the woods as being fresh and green, but marvellous changes take place within the next few weeks. The trees and shrubs, in turn, gradually assume their gorgeous autumn colouring till the woods display a multitude of shades of grey, yellow, russet, brown, red, crimson, and even violet, mingled here and there with the sombre dark bluish-green of the pines and firs. Then commences, and continues, the fall of the leaf, so that long before the autumn is at an end all is leafless with the exception of the evergreen trees and shrubs. These two phenomena—the changes in the colour of the foliage and the fall of the leaf—are of such vast interest and importance that we must devote a separate chapter to each.

# CHAPTER XVI

# AUTUMN TINTS

O many the woods in autumn possess but few attractions. The temperature is not so genial as that of late summer. The autumn winds, often chilly and boisterous, usually bring so much rain that the ground is sodden, and all vegetation dripping with moisture. Even when the weather is fine, the heavy dews of night render everything as wet as if drenching showers of rain had fallen, and the hours of sunshine are so reduced, and the slanting rays of the low sun so feeble, that the ground and the vegetation often retain their moisture throughout the day. The disappearance of most of the wild flowers also decreases the attractiveness of the woods.

But the lover of nature looks on all these things from his own point of view. He finds the cool and boisterous winds highly invigorating. In the absence of the sun, he delights in the swift-drifting clouds. Suitably clad and shod, he defies the drifting rain, the dewy grass, and the dripping trees. And, in the almost total absence of flowers, he glories in the lovely autumn tints displayed by the forest trees and shrubs, tints which are also assumed by many of our low-growing herbs.

Now let us see if we, too, can appreciate these autumn colours, and inquire somewhat into their meaning and significance.

Standing at some little distance from a wood, we are struck by the wonderful variety of tints displayed by the various trees—the yellowish-brown foliage of the oak, and the rich tawny brown of the beech, broken here and there by the pale yellow of the birch, the glaucous green of the firs, and the dark bluish-green of the pines, further relieved, on the outskirts of the wood, by the scarlets and purples of the mountain ash and the wild cherry, and the variety of tints displayed by the bordering bushes and shrubs.

Equally interesting is the coppice of underwood and small shrubs. Here we find the ubiquitous bramble, so familiar that it claims but little attention now that its fruiting season is over. But look at its foliage. Some of its leaves are still green; but others are yellow or orange, and many are of a rich puce, purple, or crimson. Sometimes we find all, or nearly all, these tints blended together in one single leaflet.

Above this we see the yellowish-brown leaves of the hazel, the pale yellow foliage of the maple, and frequently the violet foliage of the spindle tree, and the blood-red stems of the dogwood. Sometimes all these tints are further blended with the yellow of the hornbeam and the birch, or relieved by the beautiful scarlet of the mountain ash and the rich purple of the bird-cherry and the wild service-tree.

Then, in the low-lying, marshy parts of wood or copse, we note the silvery-white foliage of the white poplar, the grey of the other poplars and of the willows, intermixed with the orange of the aspen and the dull brownish-green of the alder.

On a sunny day in mid-autumn, when most of the trees in a wood are partially or completely denuded, we often observe that the trunks of the trees and the under sides of the lower branches appear unusually light, with a distinct yellowish glow. This is particularly noticeable in beech woods, and is due to the fact that the light of the sun falling on the carpet of golden-orange leaves is reflected upwards. A similar effect is produced in some woods by the reflection of sunlight from dense masses of yellow-brown bracken.

It is a pleasure to witness such glorious scenes, knowing or caring naught as to the true significance of the wonderful variety of colouring, or as to the causes which give rise to them; but this pleasure is considerably enhanced when one can understand somewhat the changes that take place in the leaves to produce the autumn tints, and the reason why such changes take place every year on the approach of the cold season. Let us spend a little time looking into this matter.

The leaves of many of our trees, shrubs, and herbs can last for one season only, since they are unable to defy the winter frosts. Not only is this the case, but it is also a real advantage to the trees and plants concerned to dispose of their leaves before the cold season sets in, though the reason for this can hardly be discussed at the present time. This foliage, now no longer of service, is therefore thrown off at the commencement of the cold season; but, since green leaves contain many substances—starchy materials, albuminoids, etc.—that are very valuable to living plants, it would not do to cast them off in their green state with the stores they hold. The plants and trees, as if aware of the threatened loss, guard against the latter by absorbing from the leaves all the useful material they contain, storing it up in their woody stems or their underground root-stocks or tubers, where it is safely deposited and stored until the following spring.

This being done, the leaves are reduced to mere skeletons, their microscopic cells now containing nothing but useless residues, together with a small amount of accumulated waste matter that the plants may dispose of with advantage.

The little *chlorophyll* bodies that impart the green colour to the foliage are changed chemically so that they may be able to pass to the winter storehouse, leaving behind them only a number of minute yellow granules. Thus the leaves lose their green colour, and tend to become yellow. Sometimes, however, so little of the yellow residue is left that it has no appreciable effect on the colouring of the dead leaf, which assumes a whitish or greyish tint, instead of a yellow one, as is the case with several of the willows and poplars.

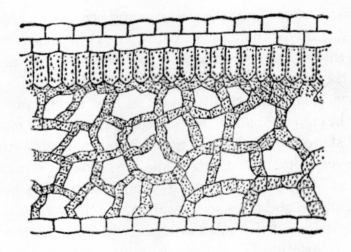

*The Cells of a Leaf, showing the chlorophyll bodies.*
*These bodies are absent in the cells of the epidermis.*

But the absorption of the nutritive materials of the leaf is not such a simple matter as would appear from the above description. The fact is that these materials have to pass through a series of very complicated chemical changes to fit them for their emigration to their winter quarters, and these chemical changes result in the formation of certain by-products that, being useless, remain in the leaves that are to be shed.

Among these by-products is a blue substance known as *anthocyanin*, and also certain vegetable acids. Now, probably, most people know that the majority of the vegetable blue colouring matters are turned red by acids. As a familiar instance of this we may recall the action of vinegar (a weak vegetable acid) on purple cabbage. The blue colouring matter of the cabbage that helps to form the purple tint is changed to red by the action of the vinegar. In a similar manner a blue or purple flower may be reddened by immersion in vinegar or any other acid, the latter, if very strong, being diluted considerably with water.

The tint of an autumn leaf depends very largely on the amount of yellow residue left behind by the emigrated chlorophyll bodies, the amount of blue colouring matter formed, and the amount of acid produced; and any one who has had a very little experience in the mixing of pigments will understand at once, from what has been said, what a variety of colours and shades may be produced in leaves by the admixture of the yellow, red, and blue pigments in varied proportions.

If only a small quantity of anthocyanin is formed, and this is turned to a pale red by acids present, the latter colour produces an orange tint when blended with the yellow residue of the chlorophyll bodies. A larger amount of the blue colouring matter, similarly reddened by the action of acids, and blended with the yellow, may produce any shade of orange-red; or, in the presence of only a very small amount of yellow residue, an almost pure red. A still larger amount of the blue colouring matter, in the presence of acids insufficient in quantity completely to redden the former, may give us crimson or any shade of purple or violet, according to the proportion in which the two materials are produced.

The blue anthocyanin is formed in varying amounts in the leaves of certain pines and firs, during the autumn; and these leaves, being evergreen, at the same time retain their chlorophyll. Thus we get a blending of green and blue, producing the dark bluish-green foliage that is so characteristic of the species referred to.

It is remarkable that anthocyanin is seldom formed in woolly or felted leaves, like those of the mullein and the wayfaring-tree; and even if it did the colour would not show through the dense covering. Hence such leaves are always grey or white when they are shed.

All who habitually observe the grand displays of autumn colouring must have noticed how variable are the seasons when these displays commence, and the periods through which they persist. As a rule, the splendour does not last very long; and it is often cut short by the sudden occurrence of October frosts, which, especially when accompanied by boisterous northerly winds, sever the tinted leaves and whirl them to the ground.

The first appearance of the autumn tints depends on the condition of the atmosphere as regards temperature and moisture. It is earliest when the September air is cool and dry, and may be late in October when the atmosphere of late summer and early autumn is warm and moist. Sometimes, when the changes in the colour of the foliage commence early in a dry September, the autumn tints will last for considerably over a month, provided there are no early frosts and northern blasts. With reversed conditions, however, the period of the display will be considerably shorter.

## CHAPTER XVII

# THE FALL OF THE LEAF

HERE are many natural phenomena with which we have been so familiar from the days of our childhood that we take them as a matter of course, without any thought of inquiring into their causes or their uses. For instance, we all observe, every autumn, that the leaves of most of our trees and shrubs, as well as those of many herbaceous plants, fall to the ground during that season; yet it never occurs to us to consider why the leaves should thus be shed, what causes them to become detached from their respective trees or plants, whether the fall of the leaf is advantageous, or even necessary for the welfare of these trees and plants, or whether it is an unfavourable process to which they are compelled to submit.

Each individual leaf of every plant or tree, like the plants and trees themselves, has its birth, growth, decline, and death. For a time each leaf is capable of performing certain very important functions; but, sooner or later, it loses the power of carrying on its work, fades, dies, and falls to the ground.

In some countries the climatic conditions are such that the vegetation can remain luxuriant and active throughout the whole of the year, and in such cases there is no definite period during which the spent-out leaves are shed, for new leaves are always forming at the tips of the branches, while the older ones, lower on the stems, are always dying and falling. With such a gradual leaf-fall the vegetation is evergreen, the trees and plants presenting the same appearance at all times.

In other countries, however, where there are well-marked seasons, it often happens that, during a certain period of each year, the conditions are such that the growth and activity of the vegetation is entirely suspended. This is the case in districts where the year consists of a wet and a dry season—a wet season during which there is a very rapid and luxuriant growth, followed by a long, dry period when no water is available for the support of vegetable life, and the foliage, now rendered useless, is shed. A similar period of general leaf-fall also marks those districts in which there is a cold winter; as this is the case with our own country, it is the one to which we shall give our attention.

First let us consider the question, "Why should the leaves fall at all in the autumn?" Now to be in a position to answer this question we should know something of the functions of leaves, and of the manner in which their duties are performed. It would be out of place to go into the details of this matter here. Suffice it to say that leaves are concerned in the building up of the organic compounds necessary for the growth of the plants, and that in the performance of this important duty they must necessarily give off large quantities of water vapour into the atmosphere. This escape of water vapour is called *transpiration*, and it may be compared with a somewhat similar function of our own skin which we call perspiration.

Of course the water expelled from the leaves comes from the moist soil, being absorbed by the root-fibres, and it is very important to note that this absorption by the roots is carried on freely when the soil is warm, and that it is greatly retarded, and may be even completely arrested, when the ground is cold.

If the leaves remained on plants and trees throughout the winter, when the activity of the roots is arrested by the low temperature of the soil, the process of transpiration would be going on, with the result that the plants concerned would be losing moisture that could not be replaced, and thus their lives would be threatened. This, then, is one reason why the leaves *must* fall in the autumn.

The various organs of our own bodies, in the performance of their duties, are always giving rise to waste products that would cause disease if they were allowed to accumulate, and there are within us certain organs whose duty it is to remove or *excrete* these waste materials. Now it so happens that waste products are formed in leaves—products that are of no use whatever to the plants, and which, by accumulation, would become burdensome, and even dangerous, to the vegetation. But when the leaves fall in autumn, this waste material is carried to the ground, so that the plants are periodically relieved of it. Thus we see a second reason why leaves should be shed.

But there is yet another. It is not at all an uncommon thing to see the leafless branches of trees and shrubs so heavily laden with snow that they break down under its weight. If leafless trees and shrubs can intercept such a mass of snow that they are often crushed to the ground, we can imagine what the result would be if they were still in leaf, and could thus catch an enormously greater quantity of snow. Some of the trees of our cold-temperate zone, however, do retain their leaves throughout the winter; but these appear to be specially adapted to withstand violent storms of both snow and wind, for their branches are so elastic that, though they may be severely strained and bent, they seldom snap. Moreover, these trees generally have very narrow, needle-like leaves, presenting so little surface to the storm that they would catch but little snow and wind in comparison with the majority of our forest trees had they remained in leaf. As a further illustration of the importance of this provision, we have only to recall actual instances of the enormous damage that is done to trees by early autumn snowstorms that occur before the leaves have fallen, and also similar disasters brought about by snowstorms in late spring, after the new foliage has appeared.

Now let us inquire into the cause or causes that bring about the fall of the leaf. It seems to be a very common opinion that frost is the cause; and there is some excuse for the prevalence of this opinion, for every one must have observed the showers of dead leaves that fall to the ground after a frosty night, especially if a light breeze springs up in the following morning. Yet frost is not the direct cause of leaf-fall. It certainly does tend to hasten the denuding of the trees, but, as we shall see presently, the trees had been making preparations for the shedding of their leaves before the frost came. As a proof of this statement, it is a fact that very early frosts do **not** cause leaves to fall, the trees not having made their necessary arrangements. Further, when the frosts of the season commence very late, the trees will shed their leaves before the first frosts have come.

We have spoken of preparations made by plants and trees for the coming leaf-fall. Such preparations are actually made, as if the members of the vegetable world could foresee the dangers ahead, and had the voluntary power to work for their own protection in the winter. The low autumn temperature of soil and air is undoubtedly the direct incitement to make ready for the approaching winter, though the degree of humidity of both soil and air appears to play some part in determining the time when the preparations shall proceed.

In places where the soil is moist and the atmosphere humid, as it is generally in wooded valleys, the leaves not only remain later on the trees, but also appear earlier in the spring. On the other hand, on open hilly ground the foliage falls earlier in autumn, and reappears later in spring. It is curious, too, that certain species of trees and shrubs may be deciduous in a country, like ours, that has a cold winter, and yet be evergreen in a more congenial climate. Thus the common elder sheds its foliage in the winter in Britain, but is evergreen in the south of Europe, and the plane tree, which is evergreen in its native country, became a deciduous tree on its introduction to Britain.

Now let us see what preparation our deciduous forest trees make for their coming winter sleep. In the first place we have already noted that green foliage contains quite a quantity of valuable organic substances that the tree cannot afford to lose; and that, if the leaves fell from the trees in their normal green condition, the latter would suffer a very serious loss. We have also learned that, to prevent such a waste of useful material, the trees, on the approach of the cold season, transfer the substances to which we have referred to some permanent parts of their structure, where they can be stored until they are required in the following spring and summer. This precaution is taken not only by our forest trees and our shrubs, but also by many perennial herbaceous plants, and the absorbed matter is stored in stems, roots, tubers, and other sheltered and protected parts.

The absorption of all this nutritive material converts the foliage into a dry and dead condition, so that when the leaves fall to the ground they carry with them practically nothing of any value to the plants. A trifling loss there may be, but such loss is exceedingly small when compared with the great advantages gained by the fall of the foliage. And even this small loss is

166

more apparent than real, for the fallen leaves decay and considerably enrich the soil in which the plants and trees grow.

Another preparation made in the autumn is the formation of what are called separation layers in some part or parts of each leaf—layers of minute, soft cells, the walls of which easily separate from one another.

It is remarkable that these separation layers are formed in places (the bases of leaves, and of the leaflets of compound leaves) where the structure is particularly strong and tough; the leaves could not detach themselves as they do without such a provision. You may easily prove this by cutting off the branch of a tree in early autumn, before the separation layers referred to have been formed. This branch will retain its leaves long after its parent tree becomes bare. In fact it will hold its leaves all through the winter, and well into the following summer, until at last the foliage is disintegrated by the natural process of decay.

The separation layer really consists of two distinct sets of cells—a layer of

*Compound Leaf of the Mountain Ash, showing where the separation layers are formed*

167

thin-walled cells, the walls of which separate when the layer is completely formed, and below or inside this a layer of cork. The little cells forming the layer rapidly increase by division, pushing their way into the older tissue until they completely divide it. When the growth of the layer is completed, the part is so weakened by the disunion of the old cells that the leaf is disconnected by the slightest disturbance; the scar it leaves on the stem is then left covered with a layer of cork that prevents any loss of sap, and presents such a clean-cut surface that it looks as if the leaf had been cut off with a sharp knife.

So fragile does the separation layer become through the loosening of its cells that the weight of the dead and empty leaf is sometimes alone sufficient to cause it to split asunder, but of course the fall of the leaves is considerably hastened by the wind.

Frost will assist in severing the cells by freezing the sap. As the latter is converted into ice, it expands, thus helping to push the cells asunder; but they are still held in place by the ice that is formed. When, however, the sun rises in the morning and thaws the ice, the holding power is gone, and the leaves fall in thousands. One very sharp frost occurring just after the separation layers have fully formed is often sufficient to cause the complete defoliation of a tree in the course of an hour or so during the thaw of the following morning. In fact, the effect of a sharp frost is such that the slightest touch, or the gentlest breeze, is sufficient, when the succeeding thaw sets in, to break simple leaves from their stems, and to cause compound leaves, like those of the horse-chestnut, the ash, and the mountain ash, to fall to pieces.

The shape of the scar left on the stem when the leaf falls depends on the shape of the leaf-stalk, or the base of the leaf itself if it is stalkless, and generally there is a bud or undeveloped branch immediately above the scar, for the buds are usually produced in the angle formed by the leaf and the stem above it.

*Leaf-Scars of the Ash, Horse-Chestnut, Walnut, and Sycamore*

In the horse-chestnut the scars are horseshoe-shaped, and the points in it where the bundles of vessels that carried the sap were severed appear just like the nail-holes of the horseshoe. In the syringa, the separation layer is formed some little distance up the leaf-stalk, so that a portion of the latter is left for the protection of the tender bud. In some trees with simple leaves two separation layers are formed on each stalk, one close to the stem, and the other immediately below the blade of the leaf, so that blades and stalks fall separately to the ground. In the plane tree the leaf-scar is in the form of a complete ring, for in this case the bud, instead of occupying the angle between leaf-stalk and stem, is entirely enclosed by the base of the former,

169

and is not visible at all until the leaf drops.

It is curious, too, that in some trees the leaf-fall commences at the tips of the branches, while in others the leaves at the tips of the twigs are the last to fall; in some, like the ash, the defoliation is very rapid, while in others, like the oak, it may extend through many days, and even several weeks.

# CHAPTER XVIII

# AUTUMN FRUITS

UTUMN is undoubtedly the best season for the study of wild fruits. It is true that many of the early-flowering plants, trees, and shrubs ripen their fruits rapidly, and that these fruits, or the seeds which they contained, have long since been scattered, or devoured by birds and other creatures. On the other hand, many of the fruits produced by the early flowers progress very slowly, and remain where they were formed till quite late in the year; and these, together with those of later species, are to be found in abundance during the present season.

In this chapter we shall endeavour to become acquainted with some of these autumn fruits, several of which are represented on the following pages, but it is necessary that, in the first place, we are clear as to the true meaning of the term "fruit."

Most flowers have, either in their centre or at their base, a green case, or a number of such cases, containing one or more smaller bodies. The cases are called *ovaries*, and the little bodies within them are the *ovules*. After

171

the latter have been fertilized by the pollen grains set free from the anthers, they gradually develop into seeds; at the same time, the surrounding ovary also enlarges, and often undergoes marked changes in form and colour, becoming a fruit. A fruit, then, is really the ripened ovary of a flower, enclosing the seed or seeds.

Ripened fruits differ very much in their nature. Some are soft and juicy, while others are hard and dry. In fact many are so small, dry, and seedlike that they are often called seeds, and only those who have studied them closely are able to decide which they are. Thus the so-called seeds of grasses and the "winged seeds" of the ash and the birch are in reality fruits.

Fruits are so varied in structure that it has been found convenient to classify them into groups, each group including those which resemble one another in one important feature; and so we speak of berries, nuts, pods, capsules, etc.; and the best way to study them is to collect a considerable number, and then endeavour, after a careful examination, to arrange them according to their structure. In doing this it is not absolutely necessary to know the names of the plants that produced the respective fruits, although it is certainly more pleasing to be able to call them by their names. It is a good plan, therefore, when gathering fruits, to take also a portion of each plant, in order better to identify the latter.

Among the most showy of autumn fruits are the brightly-coloured berries that are so conspicuous in our woods and hedgerows. Some of them continue to

172

display themselves till the end of the year, but many are devoured, as they ripen, by thrushes, blackbirds, starlings, and other birds. In hedgerows and copses the zigzag climbing stems of the woody nightshade or bitter-sweet bear clusters of oval berries; the twining black bryony, with scarlet berries extending for several feet along its stems, encircles the twigs of shrubs, here and there forming richly-decorated pendants and festoons; and the honeysuckle is tipped with close clusters of red berries. Here we may also see the beautiful dark red berries of the guelder-rose. Then, in shady places, close to the ground, are the dense masses of the red berries of the cuckoo-pint or wild arum, at the summit of thick, green stalks.

*Autumn Fruits (from left to right): Guelder Rose, Wild Rose, Hawthorn*

It may be mentioned here that the term "berry" should, strictly speaking, be applied only to succulent fruits containing a soft, pulpy mass in which one or more seeds are embedded. Some of our autumn fruits that are commonly spoken of as berries, and are berry-like in general appearance, are really stone-fruits, like

173

*Autumn Fruits (from left to right): Larch, Elder, Bramble*

the cherry and the plum. Among these are the dark purple fruits of the alder buckthorn bush, commonly, but of course wrongly, called the berry-bearing buckthorn; also the bright red fruits of the holly, which each contain four little "stones"; the "haws" of the hawthorn; the black fruits of the spiny sloe or wild plum, remarkable for their bluish bloom; and the "berries" of the elder, the clusters of which are so large that they bend down the twigs which bear

*Autumn Fruits (from left to right): Oak, Medlar, Sloe*

*Autumn Fruits (from left to right): Holly, Crab Apple, Ash*

174

them. Even the blackberry belongs to this section, for it is really a group of little stone-fruits clustered on a central column.

The crab apple, which is abundant in many of our woods, is a type of another class of fruits called *pomes*. In this the core is the real fruit—the ripened ovary of the flower—and the surrounding fleshy substance is formed by the tube of the calyx, which completely encloses the core; on the top of the apple can be seen the withered remains of the divisions of the calyx. In the south of England we often meet with the wild pear and the wild medlar trees, the fruits of which are also pomes, but in the latter the core is visible at the top, where the divisions of the calyx are much larger and more distinct than in the apple and the pear.

Among our common autumn fruits there are quite a large number of nuts and nutlets—hard, dry, seedlike fruits, some of which are of considerable size, while others are very minute. The largest of these are the sweet-chestnut and the horse-chestnut, both of which are to be found in woods and plantations, but it is interesting to note that neither of the trees producing these is truly British, but that both were introduced, the former

*Autumn Fruits (from left to right): Pine, Chestnut, Buckthorn*

175

*Autumn Fruits (from left to right): Sycamore, Honeysuckle, Yew*

from Southern Europe, and the latter from Greece or Persia. There is a difference between these two fruits that would be regarded as important by the botanist, and which may be of some interest to the general reader. The sweet-chestnuts are true nuts, enclosed in a prickly, green "cupule" which is not really a part of the fruit, but rather a covering formed from the calyx of the flower. The horse-chestnuts, on the other hand, are seeds rather than fruits, and the spiny green covering is the ripened ovary of the flower.

We have other examples of nuts in cupules, like that of the sweet-chestnut. The beech tree produces triangular nuts that are completely surrounded by a bristly cupule; the acorn has an open, rough cupule at its base; the cupule of the hazel nut is thin and leafy; and the corresponding structure of the little nut of the hornbeam tree is not in the form of a cup, but lies only on one side.

Some of our forest trees produce nuts that are not enclosed in cupules. The fruits of the ash are little nuts the outer shells of which are extended into long, narrow wings; and those of the birch are two-winged, very minute nuts. The fruits of the alder are little nuts that drop from between the woody scales of "cones" which look something like fir cones. The elm tree produces winged nuts, but these are ripened very early in the year, so that we shall not find them during the present season.

In addition to all the above, a very large number of our shrubs and herbs produce nutlets, most of which are very small, and nearly always spoken of as seeds. Daisies, hawkweeds, mayweeds, thistles, dandelions, borage, dead-nettles, docks, stinging-nettles, sedges, and a host of other plants have such fruits.

Hitherto we have said nothing about fruits which split when ripe, with the exception of the fruit of the horse-chestnut tree; but we meet with quite a number of these in the autumn.

Some of them are pods, like the well-known pea-pod, which splits into two parts and has its seeds all attached along one seam. We see them on the broom and furze of heath and moor, on the vetches of hedges and thickets, and on the bird's-foot trefoil and the meadow vetchling of dry fields; but many of them have long since cast their seeds, and nothing now remains save the dried empty valves of the pods, often twisted into a spiral form.

A very similar kind of fruit will be found on the wild mustards, cresses, and rockets, but these are divided internally by a central membrane which gives attachment to the seeds on *both* sides. Although often called pods, they are really *siliquas*. A short, triangular

*The Shepherd's Purse*

fruit of this description may be seen on the shepherd's-purse all through the year.

On the columbine of our thickets and the wild larkspur of corn-fields we see yet another podlike fruit (*follicle*), but in this case there is a seam on one side only.

Then hundreds of our wild flowers produce splitting fruits, of all shapes and sizes, called *capsules*. These may have two or more seams. Some of them split at the top only, like the capsules of the campions and the catchfly; others split throughout their length, as the capsules of the mullein, foxglove, and evening-primrose. Some split transversely, like the globular fruit of the pretty little scarlet pimpernel, while others split in such a manner that they give rise to one or more holes through which the seeds may escape, as is the case with the poppy-head, and the fruits of the bell-flowers and the snapdragon.

In our woodland rambles we cannot help noticing the very conspicuous fruits (cones) of the pines, firs, and larches. These do not belong to any of the groups previously mentioned, but are of a very exceptional nature, for the seeds here are not enclosed in ovaries, like those of the other plants and trees, but simply lie on the woody scales of the cone. It is for this reason that the pines and firs are commonly spoken of as the naked-seeded trees. The yew is always included in this group of trees, although it does not bear a woody cone. Its fruit consists of a single seed, partly embedded in a beautiful semi-transparent, bright red, juicy cup.

It is an interesting hobby to make a study of the fruits of our wild herbs and trees by collecting all that are seen, examining their structure, and then grouping them accordingly. And although the autumn season yields the different kinds of fruits in the greatest profusion, yet the study should not be confined to the fall of the year, for many of the spring and early summer flowers produce their fruits rapidly, and the latter fall or otherwise disappear long before the autumn commences.

# CHAPTER XIX

# THE DISPERSION OF SEEDS AND FRUITS

 OME herbs yield thousands of seeds, and, in the case of our forest trees, the number produced by a single individual may run into many tens of thousands or even many hundreds of thousands. The poppy, the foxglove and the mullein raise long spikes of fruits, each of which contains a very large number of minute seeds. The elm and the ash bear, in their respective seasons, thousands of dense clusters of fruits, each containing a seed. The beech and the oak often shed sufficient nuts to cover almost completely the ground beneath them, and each birch tree produces thousands of catkins of closely-packed, minute one-seeded fruits.

Now, if there were no natural means by which seeds were scattered, and all were simply dropped beneath the parent plant or tree, it is clear that very few of them could ever give rise to mature offspring. Even allowing for the large number that would be devoured by animals or otherwise destroyed, the seedlings that followed would generally be so crowded that they would choke one another in their struggle for existence, and only a few survivors, if any, would ever reach maturity.

But Nature has provided means for the dispersion of seeds, and during our autumn rambles we can hardly find a more interesting occupation than the study of the different ways in which this is accomplished. We must mention, however, as in the case of the study of fruits, that although late summer and autumn are the best seasons for this employment, yet many plants and trees shed their seeds earlier in the year.

Some seeds are so small that, in the mass, they form a fine dust such as can be carried considerable distances by even a gentle breeze. This is the case with orchids, the seeds of which are scattered by the wind as soon as the capsules open. The minute *spores* of mosses, ferns, fungi, and other flowerless plants are similarly scattered. In these plants the dustlike spores take the place of seeds in reproducing the species.

Other larger seeds are especially adapted to the same means of distribution. Those of the wallflower are flattened, and their outer walls are extended to form thin wings. Again, when the cones of pines and firs are ripe, their woody scales separate, and the wind blows out the winged seeds that lie between them. These seeds may be obtained by breaking up a ripe cone, or even by tapping it gently.

As a rule it is not simply the seed that is scattered by the wind or other agency, but the complete fruit—the seed together with covering or ovary, and many fruits are wonderfully adapted for wind-distribution. The winged fruits of the elm are scattered in abundance during the spring, but at the present time winged fruits are to be seen on the birch, ash, maple, and sycamore. Take a fruiting catkin from the birch tree, roll it gently between finger and thumb, and an enormous number of tiny fruits will drop, each one with a double wing. The ash fruit is much larger, and has a large wing at one end. This wing is slightly twisted, like the blade of a propeller; consequently, when the fruit falls from its tree, it does not go straight to the ground, but spins rapidly, thus retarding its descent, and giving the breeze a better opportunity of carrying it far from its former home. The fruits of the maple and sycamore are also of moderate size. Both consist, usually, of two parts, each containing a seed, and each provided with a large thin wing.

The fruits of the lime and the hornbeam are both scattered by the wind, and yet they are not really winged fruits. They have, however, an attachment that

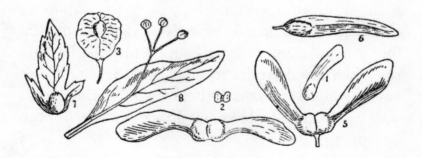

*Seed and Fruits dispersed by the wind.—Winged seed of the Pine (1); Winged fruits of the Birch (2), Elm (3), Maple (4), Sycamore (5), and Ash (6). Also fruits of the Hornbeam (7) and Lime (8).*

182

serves the same purpose as a wing. The little nut of the hornbeam lies on a three-lobed leafy scale, that adheres to it, and serves the purpose of a sail. A similar office is performed by a leafy scale attached to the fruit-stalks of the lime tree.

Quite a number of seeds and fruits have, instead of wings, a tuft of hairs that serves as a parachute, and enables the wind to carry them to a considerable distance. Look at the old flowering stems of thistles, dandelions, hawk-

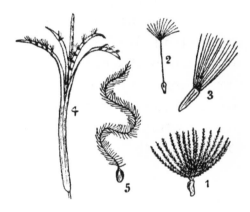

*Tufted Seeds and Fruits.—(1) Thistle; (2) Dandelion; (3) Hawkweed; (4) Willow-Herb; (5) Wild Clematis.*

weeds, and Michaelmas daisies, and you see, in place of the former flowers, globular masses of radiating silky hairs. Take a ripe head on a dry sunny day, and submit it to a strong puff of air, and numerous little nutlike fruits are blown off, each one bearing a tuft of the hairs. If there is the slightest breeze, these little fruits sail away, supported by their parachutes, until they are lost in the distance.

The parachutes close in wet or damp weather, and expand again when the atmosphere is dry. The fruits are blown from their receptacles only in dry weather, as a rule, and may be carried for miles with their parachutes open wide. If the weather changes, and the atmosphere becomes humid, the parachutes close, and the fruits drop to the ground, where they are washed into the crevices of the soil by the first shower of rain.

In some instances, notably in the thistles, the fruits are very feebly attached to their hairy tufts, and become detached by the slightest shock. If, for example, one of the fruits is blown against a tree, bush, or other obstruction, it separates from the parachute, which continues to sail away without its natural burden. This will explain how it is that such a large proportion of the silky tufts we see in the air during early autumn, or earlier in the year, are sailing on a fruitless voyage.

In a few of our wild plants and trees we have examples of tufted seeds, rather than fruits. The willow-herbs, for instance, have long, podlike capsules that split into four "valves," and liberate a number of tiny seeds with silky tufts. Early in the year, too, the capsules of poplars and willows set free little seeds that are enveloped in a cottony down.

One of the most conspicuous features of the hedgerow in autumn is the dense white clusters of the fruits of the wild clematis—clusters which have earned for the climber the name of "old man's beard." Looking at these closely we find that there are numerous little seedlike fruits collected into groups, each fruit bearing a long filament thickly clothed with hairs and looking like a slender, curled feather. These feathery appendages enable the fruits to be carried considerable distances on windy days.

Many of the fruits which split when ripe contain

seeds that are neither winged, tufted, nor plumed, and it would seem, at first sight, that they must fall directly below the parent plant, or nearly so, as soon as they are free. But this is not the case, for although the seeds are such that they could not be carried far by the direct force of the wind, they are, for the most part, thrown from their fruits as the latter are swayed by a strong breeze, and thus are fairly well distributed, even though within a limited range. Some of the fruits referred to, however, open in such a manner that only a strong wind can dislodge the seed, and so the range becomes wider.

Note, for instance, the poppy capsule, which opens by forming small holes, only round the top; the capsule of the wild snapdragon, which has two or three holes

*Fruits of the Poppy (1), Snapdragon (2), and Bell-Flower (3)*

near the top; and that of the wild bellflowers, with holes at the top or side.

Walking through rough herbage in autumn we often find that our garments become decorated with a variety of fruits which cling tenaciously. These will include the little fruits of the goose-grass or cleavers, each of which consists of two rounded lobes covered with hooked spines; the seedlike fruits of various grasses that cling by means of their rough scales and bristles; and the fruit-clusters of the agrimony, geum or avens, and the burdock, all of which are provided with hooked spines. These and other similar fruits are distributed by

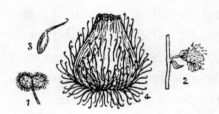

*Fruits distributed by animals.—*
*(1) Goosegrass; (2) Agrimony;*
*(3) Avens; (4) Burdock.*

the agency of animals, to whose wool, fur, or feathers they will cling for some considerable time. It is quite a common thing to see the wool of sheep that have been feeding in rough pastures laden with hundreds of clinging fruits, which are often carried long distances before they become detached.

Many birds help considerably in the distribution of seeds in quite a different way. They devour berries of various kinds, and afterwards drop the seeds which they contained, the latter being undigested and quite uninjured in their passage through the birds' bodies. Squirrels, jays, and nutcrackers also take part in the work of distribution, for they lay up winter stores of nuts and other fruits which are often forgotten and left to germinate in the hiding-places.

Water also assists in the scattering of the seeds and fruits of aquatic and semi-aquatic plants, as well as of those plants and trees which grow on the banks of streams. And even the rain does its share of the work of distribution. In fact some fruits and seeds seem to be specially adapted to secure the aid of the running stream and the shower of rain. Thus the fruits of some sedges and rushes that grow on river banks, and the seeds of water-lilies, have cells or spaces filled with air to render them buoyant, so that they may keep afloat for some time. Again, the fruits of the yellow stonecrop, that grows on walls and rocks, keep their walls closed during fine weather, so that their seeds may not be blown to unfavourable spots. Then, when the rain comes, the fruits open, and the little seeds are washed into crevices where they can grow best. Those species of speedwell which grow only close to water or in marshes also prevent their seeds from being scattered by the wind, but allow them to be washed into the wet soil of the immediate neighbourhood by rain.

But perhaps most interesting of all, as far as seed-distribution is concerned, are the mechanical contrivances by which seeds are forcibly thrown from the parent plant.

Wandering among the furze on a warm, sunny day you hear on all sides a quick succession of crackling sounds as if something were snapping. You approach a furze bush to investigate the matter, and the probability is that seeds, thrown with considerable force, as by a catapult, strike you in the face.

This is due to the fact that the seed-pods, as they ripen and dry, gradually become greatly strained, and at last burst with such force that the seeds are thrown far away. Many pods burst in this manner, including those of the broom and various vetches; and the slinging force of the valves of the pod is usually increased greatly by a sudden twisting or curling at the moment of their separation.

As another example of "explosive fruits" we may mention that of the wild balsam, to be found in shady woods in early autumn. This fruit has five valves,

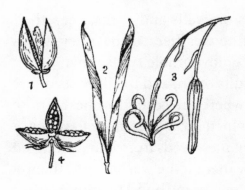

*Slinging and Explosive Fruits.*
*(1) Furze; (2) Vetch;*
*(3) Balsam; (4) Violet.*

and, when ripe, the tension is so great that the valves suddenly snap asunder, and curl up, slinging the seeds in all directions. Further, when the ripe fruits are touched, the tension is suddenly released, even while they are yet green. This characteristic serves a useful purpose, for when the living creatures of the woods brush against the fruits, the latter explode, slinging their seeds into the fur or feathers of the animals, who carry them far from the parent plant.

Quite a large number of our wild fruits sling away their seeds in various ways, but the mention of one other must suffice. The fruits of the wild violets are composed of three valves. When ripe, the valves separate, and spread themselves, while the seeds still remain attached. Each valve is now shaped like a little boat, and contains a double row of round, smooth seeds. As the fruit dries, the opposite walls of the valves approach one another, pressing against the seeds. This pressure shoots the seeds out, one by one, with considerable force, just as a pea or an orange pip may be shot by pressing it between finger and thumb.

It is interesting to collect various explosive and other slinging fruits, and to place them on a large sheet of white paper spread in the sunshine; this gives an opportunity of watching their action, and of noting the distances to which the seeds are propelled.

When dealing with the different kinds of fruits we recommended the collection of these for the instructive purpose of noting their structure and classifying them accordingly. Now we recommend another very instructive employment—that is, to make a second collection, and arrange them in groups according to the method by which their seeds are dispersed. Such collections are useful for future study.

# CHAPTER XX

# HOW ANIMALS PREPARE FOR THE WINTER

ANY of the living creatures with which we become familiar during our spring and summer rambles are very short-lived, and never survive the winter. This is the case with some species of spiders, and many of the flies, butterflies, moths, wasps, bees, and other insects. These creatures, of course, have to arrange for the perpetuation of their species before they die, and so they lay the eggs that are to give rise to the next generation before the cold weather sets in.

Of the other animals, which live from one year to another, some remain active all through the winter, while others pass a part or the whole of the cold season in a state of torpidity. These latter are spoken of as hibernators.

Why should there be this difference in the mode of spending the winter months? The answer is that it is almost entirely a matter of food supply. For instance, most insects could not remain active through the winter because there are no wild flowers to provide nectar to those who subsist on it, and little or no carrion for those which live on decomposing matter. And since the insects either die or pass the winter in seclusion, while at the same time the worms of the soil burrow more deeply to avoid the frosts, frogs and toads, that subsist on insects and worms, are also deprived of winter food. Again, as frogs have now retired to secluded places for their winter sleep, snakes, which feed almost entirely on frogs, are also deprived of their means of subsistence. It must be remembered that no animal could live through a prolonged period of activity without taking food, for the wear and tear of an active life means a loss to the body which must be replenished.

It is commonly supposed that animals hibernate because they cannot withstand the low temperature of the cold winter months. This may be true to some extent, but it is certain that several at least of the hibernators may be exposed to many degrees of frost for some time without the slightest injury.

Some of our hibernating quadrupeds make their winter homes in places that are not secure from severe frosts. Frogs may be embedded in a block of ice or in frozen mud for several days, or even weeks, and then, on the return of warm weather, creep out of their hiding-places without showing any signs of discomfort. And some insects pass the winter, either in the chrysalis stage or as perfect insects, with full exposure to the winter winds, snows, and frosts.

Several of our wild quadrupeds can find the food

they require all through the winter. The fox can always manage to find a rabbit, a wounded pheasant or partridge, or a chicken or other delicacy in a neighbouring farmyard. The carnivorous stoat and weasel have no difficulty in securing field-mice, rats, and, towards the end of the winter, young rabbits. The mole, though it may have to burrow deeper in frosty weather, is always able to find its favourite worms and grubs. The rabbit has a plentiful supply of herbage except when there are heavy snows, and then it can feed on the bark of young trees. The field-vole, sometimes called the short-tailed field-mouse, can always find herbage and roots. And the omnivorous rat never fails to find or steal a satisfactory meal when it is hungry.

The squirrel may be termed a winter-hider or a partial hibernator, for it does not spend the whole of the cold season in a state of unbroken torpidity. During the autumn it gathers nuts and other food, stores it in various hiding-places, and then, when the cold season commences, goes to sleep in some snug retreat. At any time, during the winter, when the weather is mild and genial, the squirrel will awake, run about actively, and partake of some of its stored food, retiring again to its winter home as the weather becomes less propitious.

The long-tailed field-mouse and the pretty little dormouse are both partial hibernators. The former lays up a store of grain, seeds, and nuts in its subterranean burrow, and goes to sleep near it on the advent of the first sharp frost, but it awakes and feeds whenever the rays of a warm sun penetrates to its retreat. The dormouse, which is purely nocturnal in its habits, prepares a snug, globular nest of fine twigs, leaves, grass, and moss, puts in a small store of seeds and fruits, and then retires: but it awakes and feeds on mild days.

Other creatures are true hibernators, retiring on the first approach of cold weather, laying up no stores of any kind, and remaining in a state of torpor until the spring sun is warm enough not only to arouse them from their deep sleep, but also to call forth the animal life or the vegetation that constitutes their food.

Shrews, which feed on insects and worms, retire to their underground homes, and the harvest mouse also makes a snug retreat beneath the soil. The hedgehog constructs a globular winter home of moss and leaves in a hole of some hedge or bank, and bats retire to hollow trees, outhouses, church-towers, etc., where they lie dormant for five months or more.

We observe that birds make no special preparations for the winter months. They can nearly always find sufficient of their natural food except when the ground is covered with snow, and very few of them make the least attempt at laying by winter stores; but a few species, the robins in particular, approach the habitations of man in hard weather, by which action they secure not only a more satisfactory shelter from inclement weather, but also bits and scraps intentionally or otherwise thrown within their reach.

There are not many reptiles in our country—only two species of snakes, and four kinds of lizards, the latter including the interesting little slow-worm or blind-worm, which is really a lizard without legs, but all these hibernate throughout the winter. They may be seen at large on warm, sunny days up to about the end of October, but rarely later. The lizards seek winter homes in holes of hedges and banks, usually selecting dry situations more or less sheltered from rain by shrubs or trees. Snakes retire into holes of similarly protected spots, often choosing the burrow of a rabbit or other small quadruped, or the base of a hollow tree, where several will often congregate and coil themselves together in a confused mass.

Frogs, toads, and newts also retire in or about October, the time varying with the nature of the season. Frogs bury themselves in soft mud, often under several inches of water. Here they remain in a perfectly dormant condition till about the beginning of March, a large number generally huddled closely together. In such a position their temperature is always very low, but it is only in the severest weather that they are actually frozen in. Toads select drier, but not dry, places for their winter sleep. Sometimes they merely push themselves underneath soft, damp soil, or they will shelter themselves in a hollow tree or in any hole or crevice they may find. Newts hibernate in holes and under stones, and not unfrequently they seek a winter home in the cellars or outhouses of human dwellings.

We have already referred to the fact that some of our most beautiful butterflies spend the winter in the perfect or winged condition. These emerge from the chrysalis during the summer, and appear on the wing during the sunny days of early autumn, but as soon as the cold and cloudy weather sets in they go under shelter, sometimes in hollow trees, and very frequently in outhouses, and even in the rooms of country dwellings. It is not at all uncommon to see one or more of these butterflies in an upper corner of a first- or second-storey room. Here they will remain perfectly motionless for days and weeks together, and if they are touched on a very cold day they appear to be quite dead; yet on one of those warm and bright days, such as we often get in late autumn and winter, they regain their vitality, fly to the window panes, and get out if possible to search, in vain, for their favourite flowers. But the short day soon becomes chilly, and the butterflies seek the nearest favourable shelter to renew their sleep.

Many insects pass the cold season in the grub or caterpillar state, or in the chrysalis stage. Some of them are exposed whenever we dig the

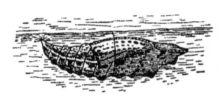

*The Chrysalis of the Large White Butterfly*

soil of our garden during this period. Others merely hide themselves among fallen leaves, or burrow at the roots of the trees on which they fed in the summer. A few even pass the winter in no better shelter than that afforded by a wall or fence, like the chrysalis of the common white cabbage butterfly, which may be seen attached to wall or garden-fence by means of a little silken carpet at its hindmost end, and a thin but strong sling of silk round its middle.

We can refer to only one other class of hibernating creatures—the slugs and snails. These, in autumn, conceal themselves under dead leaves, logs, or stones; or find a ready-made hole where a large number may often be seen together. Most of the snails close the mouths of their shells by means of thin, parchment-like membranes, composed of the dried slime from their bodies mixed with a small amount of limy material. Some of them leave a small hole in this membrane for the exchange of air, and it is probable that, where this precaution is not taken, sufficient air for the winter sleep passes through the substance of the membrane itself.

## CHAPTER XXI

# FIELDS AND HEDGEROWS
# IN AUTUMN

 IELD-PATH rambles in autumn are certainly not so interesting as in the previous season. Scarcely a wild flower is to be seen, and the fruits of the summer flowers have been mostly trodden down or devoured by sheep and cattle. Even the meadow grasses have all done flowering, and have shed their fruits, with the exception of the annual meadow grass, which may still be seen in flower.

The bordering hedges are decidedly more attractive, for they still give shelter to a few conspicuous flowers, while their bushy summits are often prettily decorated with various autumn fruits. These latter, however, are

*The Annual
Meadow Grass*

197

usually equally at home in woods and thickets, and have already been noted in a previous chapter.

Yet the pasturage still presents some interesting features. The abundance of mole-hills at this season is unusually striking, and it is instructive to watch the tunnelling operations of the mole as it extends its underground passages in search of worms and grubs.

Stepping very gently among the mole-heaps, here and there pausing to take a careful survey of the surrounding ground, we see a spot where the turf is pushed slightly upward by an upheaving force below.

*The Mole*

This is where the mole is pushing itself forward through the soft soil, aided by its pointed snout and its powerful fore-limbs. At another point we observe the upheaval of loosened soil as the mole, burrowing at a greater depth, throws up a heap of mould to clear its subterranean "run." In either case the sound of a footstep warns the creature of threatened danger; the work instantly ceases, and the mole rapidly retreats to a safer distance.

It is remarkable that the mole has its regular times for feeding, taking its meals at about eight o'clock in the morning, at noon, and again about four hours later. Hence these are the best hours in which to study the burrowing operations.

In most fields, and particularly those in the neighbourhood of woods and bushy wastes, we notice quite a network of irregular tracks in the grass, usually about three or four inches wide, where the herbage is trodden down or cropped close to the ground. These are the tracks made by rabbits during the night, or in some cases, by hares, but the tracks of the latter are usually much less irregular than those of the rabbit.

Following one of these tracks we see, here and there, points at which it is interrupted by tufts of longer grass or coarse herbage. These are places in which the rabbits met with obstructions when first establishing the run— obstructions formed by coarse vegetation which they did not want to eat; they always jump over these as they follow their beaten track. It is in these tracks that farmers place the wire snares so often used for catching rabbits.

Rough pastures are often of greater interest to a lover of nature than the well-kept meadow, for they generally produce a greater variety of wild flowers, and a coarse or bushy vegetation that affords abundant shelter to birds and other wild creatures. Here we shall find not only several species of late flowers, but also a variety of the earlier flowering plants now in fruit.

In these rough pastures we get splendid opportunities of learning some of the means adopted by plants to protect themselves from the attacks of animals. While the grass and other sweet herbage has been cropped close to the soil, there are conspicuous tufts and clumps, here and there, of plants and shrubbage which the grazers have left to flourish uninjured.

Hedgerows, waste grounds, and the borders of cultivated fields are full of interest during the early part of autumn, especially if they are in sheltered positions with a southern aspect. In such places we may see the pretty herb Robert—a species of wild geranium, bearing pink flowers; the white dead-nettle, with leaves somewhat resembling those of the stinging-nettle in form, but bearing whorls of rather large white, lipped flowers; the red dead-nettle, with smaller purple-red

*The Herb Robert*  *The White Dead-Nettle*

flowers; yellow hawkweeds; the spotted persicary; and the petty spurge, whose yellowish-green flowers are almost of the same colour as the leaves.

*The Red Dead-Nettle*       *The Petty Spurge*

In addition to these we are almost sure to see a few other common weeds that flower more or less freely all the year round.

Passing by hedgerows and banks we can hardly fail to notice the variety of tints displayed by the autumn foliage of the low-growing plants—the yellow, purple-brown, and red of the bramble leaves, the scarlet of leaves and stems of the herb Robert, the richly variegated tints of the foliage of the creeping ivy, the yellows and browns of the withering leaves of various herbs, the rich russet of the bracken, all mingled with the different shades of green still retained by grasses, ferns, and other perennial plants.

Here, too, at this season, though evidences of animal life are rapidly decreasing, we may still see the watchful little lizard basking in the warm sunshine of a bright day, and hear its rustle as it scampers away to its hiding-place. But the holes leading to the nests of wasps and wild bees no longer present their former scene of activity. The hurried ingress and egress has now ceased, and the nests may be dug out for examination with impunity, for the occupants have all died with the exception of the hibernating queens who are now commencing their long winter sleep.

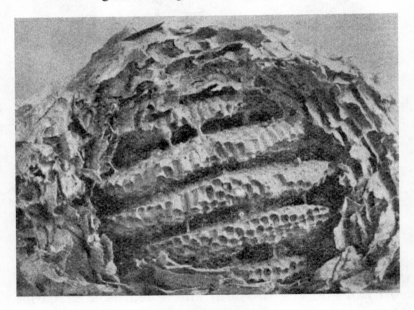

*A Discarded Wasps' Nest*

# WINTER

## CHAPTER XXII

# THE WINTER CONDITION
# OF PLANTS

E have already seen how trees and shrubs prepare for the winter—how they form the buds that are to produce the branches, leaves, and flowers of the following year, how they abstract from their leaves the valuable nutrient matter they contain, and store it in their stems, and how they then arrange for the shedding of the delicate leaves which could not withstand the frosts and storms of the cold season, and which, if allowed to remain, would only be a source of loss and danger. And now, during our winter rambles, we observe that the trees and shrubs are taking a period of perfect rest. No signs of growth are to be discerned, for the activity of the microscopic cells of which they are built has ceased as a result of the low temperature of the soil and atmosphere.

It will be interesting now to notice how the various herbs spend the cold winter months.

The herbaceous plants may be divided into three

groups—the annuals, which live for one season only; the biennials, that live through one winter and die after flowering during the following year; and the perennials, which live through several years. In all cases, the plants that remain alive through the winter spend the whole or part of this period in a state of complete rest or inactivity.

Many of our wild plants are annuals. As a rule these grow rapidly during the warm days of spring and summer; and then, after bearing their blossoms and scattering their seeds, they die completely even to the roots. Thus, for several months there remains nothing to represent them save the seeds they have left behind.

And it is remarkable that even these seeds must necessarily have a period of rest, or, as the gardener puts it, they must be allowed to ripen after they are gathered. To illustrate this, take a chestnut or an acorn, plant it in wet sawdust in the autumn, and keep it in a moderately warm room. It will not begin to sprout till the following spring, and then it will grow even if the temperature is lower than that to which the seed has been subjected all through autumn and winter.

Occasionally it happens that annual herbs cannot flower during their first season, either because the weather of that season has been unusually unfavourable, or because the plants have been cut down after they had commenced to throw up their flowering stalks. In such instances the plants will often live through the winter, and flower the next year, thus becoming biennials for the time being.

Again, annuals, and indeed other flowering plants, may often be seen in flower much later than their usual season where their growth has been interrupted by grazing animals, mowing, and hedge-trimming. By such means their flowering stage may be delayed either to the following year or only to a later period of the same year.

Many of the plants which do not flower in their first season store reserves of food-material that enable them to resume growth as soon as the severe weather of winter is over, and then they produce flowers and fruits, and die. These, of course, are biennials; but some, instead of dying in their second season, repeat this process from year to year, and become perennials. All, however, spend the cold season in a condition of rest.

During the winter months we may easily find numerous examples of the food-reserves referred to. Go to a shady bank where you have seen the daffodils in spring, and you find no traces of the plants, although they are perennials. But turn up some of the soil, and there you find the resting plants in the form of bulbs.

Each bulb contains all the parts of the plant in a rudimentary condition. At the base is a hard mass which constitutes the stem, and from which the root-fibres proceed downwards. The rest consists of fleshy scales that give rise to the future leaves and flowering stem, and which contain a store of food-material to support the plant during the early stages of the spring growth. In fact, the bulb is a resting winter-bud.

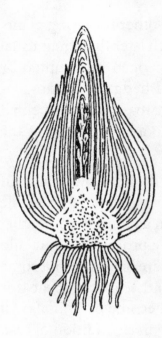

*Section of a Bulb*

Bulbs, like seeds, require a period of rest previous to the growth of the leaves and flowers. If you plant a snowdrop bulb in autumn, and keep it at a moderate temperature, it will refuse to grow until its proper season arrives; it will then develop even though the temperature be lower than that in which it spent the earlier months. It may be hastened somewhat from its sleep by a "forcing" temperature, but under such a condition a weak plant that soon perishes is the result.

Some bulbs do not adhere so rigidly to their natural period of rest, and may be "forced" to produce leaves and flowers much before the usual time. Such is the case with tulips and daffodils.

Some plants spend the winter as swollen stems that are bulb-like in form and possess one or more undeveloped buds which are termed "eyes." These stems are called tubers, and we have a familiar example in the potato.

These also contain a store of food to support the growing shoots, which proceed from the eyes, until they have their own green leaves and can manufacture the material they require. As a rule tubers are formed beneath the surface of the ground, but a visit to a damp bank where the lesser celandine grows will reveal many little tubers, that have become detached from the dead stalks, lying exposed to view.

Tubers, again, must have their season of rest—a fact that is well known to all who are acquainted with the storage of potato crops. If potatoes are kept in a deep or secluded cellar where the temperature is practically the same all the year round, they will never sprout until the usual planting season is at hand.

*Tubers of the Lesser Celandine*

Many plants have yet another way of laying up stores and resting through the winter. If we dig up some soil in a field or in any waste, weedy spot, we are sure to meet with thick "root-stocks," sometimes with a crown of leaves that remain green throughout the season; and also creeping underground stems, bearing buds. These represent plants which flourished in the summer, and then died down to the ground after storing food in their underground structures to support the new growth at the commencement of the next season. We have good examples of perennial root-stocks in the dandelion, docks, primrose, violet, willow-herbs, and the ragwort, and of creeping underground stems in couch-grass, creeping-thistle, and bindweed.

It should be mentioned here that all material required in building up a plant is manufactured in the leaves and other green parts exposed to light and air, and that this manufactured material is then conducted down to the parts in which it is to be stored. It will thus be understood that if all the green structures of a plant die at the end of a season, it is absolutely impossible for any new growth to take place in the following spring unless there is a food-reserve to call upon until the spring leaves are able to provide material for the building up of new tissues.

During the winter nearly all the tall stems and

*Winter Condition of the Foxglove*

flower-stalks of herbs die down, but in some cases the lower leaves remain alive and green all through the season. If the upper parts did not die they would surely be broken down during the winter storms, and as to the lower leaves which remain alive, they generally lie close to the ground, where they are sheltered from high winds, and spread themselves horizontally in such a manner that several inches of snow could do them no injury.

*Winter Condition of the*
*Mullein*

*Winter Condition of the*
*Bitter-Cress*

## CHAPTER XXIII

# TREES IN WINTER

T would be a great mistake to suppose that our forest trees no longer possess any points of interest when they have lost their leaves. They still present many important features deserving close attention, and there are still many things to be learned about them. Some of the features to which we refer might have attracted notice while the trees were in leaf, but are now rendered more conspicuous by the absence of the foliage.

First, let us ramble among the trees and examine the bark covering their boles and their larger branches, no longer darkened by the deep shadows of dense foliage.

The boles of some trees are covered with a very thick bark, broken by longitudinal fissures that give a very rugged appearance. Sometimes the fissures are narrow, forming a series of more or less regular ridges and furrows; but often they are wavy or zigzag, surrounding angular patches of thick bark. The arrangement of the furrows, ridges, and patches is so constant in the trees

*Bole of the Chestnut*          *Bole of the Lime*

of one species that it is as easy, after a certain amount of careful observation, to recognise trees by their bark as by their leaves. The oak, lime, ash, chestnut, elm, and white willow all have rugged barks, and yet no two of these are alike in the size and arrangement of their ridges and furrows.

Other trees have a thick or moderately thick bark, so little furrowed that it may be described as smooth. Such a bark covers the boles of the sycamore, beech, holly, and hornbeam.

The conspicuous silvery bole of the birch—"the lady of the woods"—is of quite a different character. On this the smooth, white bark peels off in horizontal, membranous strips,

*Bole of the Sycamore*

213

as thin as paper, leaving darker streaks alternating with the silvery portions not yet ready to be shed. On some of the older birch boles, however, there is, at the base, a very thick and rugged bark, strongly contrasting with that above it.

The plane tree has yet another type of bark, and although this tree is seldom seen in woods, but rather in parks, gardens, and urban thoroughfares, it is deserving of notice as one that is almost sure to attract the attention of nature students. In this instance the surface is smooth, but peels every year by throwing off thin, irregular scales of outer bark, giving the bole a very patched appearance.

In young trees the bark is at first very thin and smooth, but as the stems grow a new layer is formed each season beneath that already existing, while the latter dies, and becomes a useful protective layer.

The outer bark consists of corky tissue which not only protects the living structures beneath from pressure and friction, but, being impervious to water, prevents the evaporation of the sap from the cells and vessels of these structures. It serves another useful purpose in protecting trees from the attacks of fungi (plants of the mushroom class) which live on trees by extracting their sap, frequently doing very serious injury to, and often killing, their host. These fungi are reproduced by minute spores which are blown about by the wind. If the spores come in contact with a dry, dead bark, they cannot grow, but if they touch a spot where the bark has been so injured as to expose the moist tissues beneath, they adhere, and grow at the expense of the tree.

We have seen that a new layer of bark is formed beneath the old bark every year, and that the outer layers become dead and dry. Now, as the stems increase in thickness by the addition of the new wood formed each summer, the dead bark, pushed outward, either peels off, as in the birch and the plane, or becomes broken, forming cracks or fissures, while the new layer of bark fills up the spaces beneath. It is this continued breaking of the old, dead bark, year after year, that causes the rugged appearance of the boles of the oak, ash, lime, and other trees.

It is instructive to note the thickness of the trunks of the trees we pass; and, from a little distance, to estimate roughly the heights to which the different species grow; but it must be remembered that we cannot judge of the comparative ages of different kinds of trees by either of these features, since trees are so variable in the rapidity of their growth. Some grow in height much more rapidly than others, and the thickness of the annual growth of wood is many times greater in some species than in others. Among the rapid growers we may mention the poplars, willows, alder, and birch; and, as examples of slow growth, the oak and the yew.

Here and there we meet with a very old oak or other kind of tree that is quite hollow in the trunk and yet alive. The signs of life at the present season are the supple young twigs with their sappy buds. On inspecting the rotten, crumbling wood that forms the lining of the comparatively thin wall surrounding the enormous cavity within, it appears impossible that such a tree could have sufficient vitality to produce a single leaf, but the explanation lies in the fact that the circulation of the sap takes place almost exclusively in the outer new wood and in other tissues immediately beneath the bark, while the function of the harder and older wood within is mainly that of support.

During the winter months the woodman is busy at his work in wood or coppice, cutting down under-wood for fuel and various other purposes, and mature wood for the timber-yard. The under-wood of the coppice is cut at fairly regular intervals varying with the species. Birch, alder, hazel, and other quick-growing wood is usually cut about every five or six years, while it is common to allow the oak coppice to rest for from fifteen to over twenty years.

Where trees are being felled we get opportunities

*An Oak Stem of Twenty-Five Years' Growth*

of learning something of the nature of different woods and of the ages of the trees cut down. The fresh surface of a sawn trunk reveals a number of rings of wood arranged concentrically round a central pith, and covered externally with bark. Each ring of wood represents one year's growth, for the thickness of a tree increases by the formation of a new ring of wood, just beneath the bark, every summer. Thus, by counting the rings of wood in the base of a tree-trunk, we obtain the age of the tree.

Again, the thickness of the annual rings in different trees varies considerably. Only ten or twelve rings may be found in a stem of alder or birch about six inches in diameter, while a similar stem of oak contains twice that number, and one of yew even six or eight times as many.

In all tree-stems there are numerous radiating lines passing from the pith in the centre, breaking through the annual rings, and running quite to the inner bark. They are very conspicuous in the oak and some other woods, but much less so in many species. They are known as *medullary rays* or pith rays, and consist of vessels which convey sap between the new wood and the interior of the stem. Wood sections also reveal spots where the rings have become irregular in surrounding branches or buds. These spots are termed knots, and are often very hard on account of the pressure of the surrounding growth.

The absence of leaves on the trees during the winter frequently reveals things that are hardly noticeable during the summer months. The discarded nests of birds and the homes of squirrels become very prominent. Tufts of mistletoe may be seen on the branches of oaks, poplars, and apple trees, and on some of the birches are conspicuous tufts of fine twigs called witches'-brooms, having the appearance of crows'-nests when viewed from a distance, but which are really diseases of the trees caused by a certain fungus that arrests the growth of the tree and produces an abnormal development of buds.

*Witches' Brooms on the Birch*

CHAPTER XXIV

# WINTER BUDS

 E have previously observed that the buds which open in the spring are formed during the preceding summer, while the trees are in full leaf. They do not, however, attract much attention until the trees are bare, and so they are often termed "winter buds."

These buds form one of the most interesting features of the trees in winter, and they are of so much importance that we make them the subject of a special chapter.

As regards position, the buds referred to are of two kinds—the terminal buds, which are placed at the extreme tips of the twigs, and the lateral or side buds.

*Buds of the Elm (left), Oak, Ash, Alder, and Mountain Ash (right)*

Buds of the Hazel (left),
Beech, Sycamore, Poplar,
and Lime (right)

Buds of White Willow (left),
Chestnut, Birch, Horse-Chestnut,
and Sallow (right)

The lateral buds were formed in the axils of the leaves—that is, in the angles formed by the leaves and the stems—and immediately below each one may be seen, in winter, the scar left by the fallen leaf.

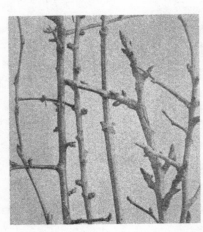

Buds of Hornbeam (left),
Sloe, Larch, Elder, Wild Cherry,
and Hawthorn (right)

In a few of our trees—the ash, sycamore, maple, and the horse-chestnut—the lateral buds are arranged in pairs, the two of each pair being exactly opposite one another; the successive pairs are alternately displaced through a right angle, so that each bud is immediately below the middle of the space

220

between the two of the pair above it. The advantage of this latter feature is evident, for when the buds give rise to leaves in the spring the leaves are never directly screened from the light of the sun by those next above them.

In other trees the buds are so placed that they run in spirals round the stem, as may be seen by passing a cotton thread from one bud to another throughout the length of a twig of one year's growth.

On a twig of the lime or the elm there are only two buds in each complete turn of the spiral, each bud being on the opposite side of the twig occupied by those next above and below it. In other words, the divergence amounts to half the circumference of a circle. On the straight twigs of the beech, alder, and hazel there are three buds to each turn of the spiral, the divergence being one-third the circumference of a circle, measured horizontally.

The bud arrangement in other trees is rather more complicated, but none the less interesting, and there is but little difficulty in tracing the spirals if well-grown straight twigs are selected for the purpose. In the oak and the broad-leaved willows, the horizontal divergence is two-fifths of the circumference of a circle, so that in *two* complete turns of the spiral there are five buds. Then, in the case of the poplar, the divergence is three-eighths of the circumference, with eight buds in *three* turns of the spiral. In the narrow-leaved willows there are thirteen buds in five revolutions of the spiral, the divergence between two adjacent buds being five-thirteenths of the circumference.

Winter buds are commonly termed "leaf-buds," because, when they open, they usually display a cluster of leaves, but they are really immature branches, some of them developing into branches which bear foliage leaves only, some into branches bearing leaves and flowers, and others into floral branches without foliage leaves. In some cases the buds that produce floral branches are larger and of a different shape as compared with those producing leafy branches on the same tree. This is notably so in some of the willows, and in orchard trees.

A longitudinal section of a large bud, such as that of the horse-chestnut, shows clearly all the parts of the future branch in embryo—the central axis or stem, the closely-folded leaves, and, in some, the clusters of flowers; the whole is enclosed in a covering of protecting scales. Of course the same structures exist in small buds, but the aid of a microscope would be necessary to enable one to distinguish the parts in these. Transverse sections of buds are also exceedingly interesting, for they enable us to see the manner in which the young leaves are folded within.

The protecting scales that envelop buds vary much in different trees. Those of the sycamore are green; of the lime, red; of the ash, black; while many are of various shades of brown. In all, the scales are impermeable to water; this is important, since a serious loss of moisture would cause a bud to die. An additional safeguard against the loss of moisture will be seen in the buds of the horse-chestnut, the scales of which are covered externally with a thick layer of a natural waterproof varnish.

No doubt the bud-scales serve other useful purposes. To a certain extent they help to keep the buds warmer than the surrounding air. Often they protect buds from the attacks of insects in early spring. In some instances they even shield the buds from birds, but there are not really many bud-scales that can withstand the sharp beaks of our feathered vegetarians.

It is remarkable that some buds grow into branches which, instead of assuming the usual form, gradually diminish in thickness till they terminate in a sharp, stiff point. Such branches are called thorns, of which we have examples in the sloe and the hawthorn. Thus thorns are to be regarded as modified branches, since both they and the normal branches have the same origin. Thorns, too, frequently resemble the latter in that they bear buds.

In addition to the visible buds which we have been considering, trees have dormant buds hidden in the living tissues beneath the bark. Such buds may remain perfectly inactive for many years; their office is to produce branches when a calamity endangering the life of the tree occurs. Thus, if a tree is broken down by a storm, and its upper portion is seriously damaged or completely destroyed, the dormant buds concealed in the trunk throw out new branches, giving the tree a new term of life.

Again, if a tree is cut down close to the ground, a

ring of new tissue is formed round the circumference of the stump, and in this ring *new* buds are formed, giving rise to fresh branches in the spring. Illustrations of this may be seen in any wood or coppice where the woodman has recently been at work.

Finally, the arrangement of the buds determines, in each species, the general form of the tree. Take a one-year-old twig from any forest tree, imagine a similar twig in the place of each bud, and we have at once an idea of the build of a two-year-old tree of that species. Continue the imaginative process, and we have a mental picture of the older tree.

If a twig has a single terminal bud, that bud continues the direction of the growth of the twig during the following season, and the branch grows straight, or with only slight curves, as with the ash, poplars, willows, hazel, etc. If, however, there are several buds clustered at the tip of a twig, as is the case with the oak, it is clear that the new growth will turn in as many different directions, and that the same thing will occur every year. This will account for the gnarled or twisted forms of the branches of an oak tree.

Eye observations of the general form and branching of trees do not quite coincide with the results which ought to obtain in accordance with the foregoing remarks, *e.g.* the branches of the sycamore are not always in pairs, the branches of hazel and ash are often forked or make a decided bend, and the branches of the oak show no evidence of radiating growths for each year. That is because only a few of the thousands of buds produced on each tree every season develop into old branches. Some are killed by sharp frosts, especially the late frosts which come after the buds begin to open; many are broken off as the twigs are hurled against one another by the winter winds; and many are destroyed by insects and birds. Making sufficient allowance for these destructive agents, it will be found that the arrangement of buds on the twig does determine the *general* form of the future tree.

# CHAPTER XXV

# ANIMAL LIFE IN WINTER

NIMAL life is now at its minimum, and during our winter rambles we shall meet but little with the exception of the non-hibernating quadrupeds, and the birds which are always in evidence.

In wooded districts we not unfrequently surprise a fox; for although this creature is generally nocturnal in its habits, often hiding in a rabbit-burrow or in an "earth" of its own excavating during the day, yet it frequently lives out, and may be disturbed unintentionally by those who stray from the usual beaten tracks. Nor is it in woods only that we may see this beautiful creature, for it will often spend the day in a tuft of coarse vegetation on rough, open ground, or in a dry ditch bordering a field or pasture. In unfrequented districts it will often hunt for its prey—rabbits, hares, partridges, etc.—during the day, but in the neighbourhood of farms and villages it will hunt (or steal) after darkness sets in; its yelping bark is then one of the few sounds breaking the silence of the night.

Weasels and stoats, although partially nocturnal in their habits, may be seen at large during any part of the day. The former, distinguished by their rich brown colour above and the pure white beneath, travel rapidly by a series of jumps, every now and then darting into holes in search of rats, mice, shrews, moles, and other prey, and it surprises one to see into what small holes they can rapidly glide their slender snake-like bodies.

Stoats are rather larger than weasels. Their colour above is a duller brown, and below they are decidedly yellowish. Their habits are very similar to those of the weasels; but, being stronger, they attack larger animals, including farmyard poultry. One may frequently hear the piercing cry of a rabbit that has been captured by a stoat. Sometimes the cry is a muffled one issuing from the burrow of the unfortunate prey; although a rabbit is usually attacked in its underground home, the struggling pair generally reach the open, where the stoat is actually dragged by the superior bodily strength of the rabbit, who endeavours to escape. This superior strength, however, is usually of no avail against the deadly grip of the stoat's jaws. Stoats, like many other carnivorous animals, delight in the hunt, and will kill even though they require no food; thus we meet with dead rabbits, wounded in the throat, from which stoats have simply sucked some blood, leaving the carcase to be devoured by other creatures.

On a bright, sunny winter's day the squirrel awakes from its slumber, and scrapes away the dead leaves and surface soil in spots where it has secreted certain of its stores of food; then, after partaking of its meal and indulging in a light frolic, it retires to its winter resting-place before the sun goes down.

As to rabbits, they are abundant everywhere, and it is remarkable that they make their appearance in many new places early in winter. This extension of range is really the result of numerous family quarrels. During the warm weather rabbits live out to a great extent, and as there is then plenty of green food to supply all wants, the families live peaceably together. But when the cold season comes with its storms and frosts, these creatures spend much time in their burrows, which now become overcrowded as a result of the numerous offspring reared in the previous spring and summer. Food, too, is now less plentiful, and to reduce these difficulties of housing and food-supply the parents drive away their youngsters to seek new homes and pastures, though we fear it often happens that the latter are victors in the family fights, and succeed in forcing the parents to leave their old homes.

Many of our well-known feathered friends are summer visitors, and these have all returned, some long time since, to warmer countries, to obtain the insects and other food which our land no longer supplies, but the "residents" greet us everywhere in our rambles abroad, and now and again we meet with winter visitors that have recently arrived here from their northern summer abodes.

Of course some of the resident birds must necessarily change their mode of living to a certain extent on account of the difficulties of food supply. Thus many of those which fed entirely or principally on insects and grubs during the summer months have now to adopt a vegetable diet, looking for their sustenance chiefly among the berries and other fruits still remaining on the hedgerows and in the woods, and among the winter buds of various trees and shrubs. We notice, too, that some species assemble in large flocks after their family cares are all over for the present year, also that our favourite songsters no longer sing as they did in spring and summer, but emit only their call-notes and their notes of alarm. Yet we may sometimes hear the song of the skylark long before the winter is over, and with increasing frequency as the spring approaches.

Very large flocks of skylarks may now be seen feeding on pastures, and frequently moving from place to place, but these are mostly birds that pay us a winter visit from the Continent, for the British skylarks seem to keep in pairs or in very small parties throughout this season.

Conspicuous, too, are the large flocks of rooks, now living far away from the rookeries, and congregating on cultivated land for their morning and evening meals. These flocks begin to break up in February, when the birds return to their rookeries, and often begin to build their nests before the winter is over.

In our woodland rambles we sometimes disturb resting birds of a brownish colour, barred with darker brown and black, about the size of a pigeon, but possessing a short tail and a long, slender beak—birds which rise with an owl-like flight, emitting a deep note followed by a sharp whistling sound. These birds are woodcocks, which visit us from the north in large flocks, and then disperse. They live for the time a somewhat solitary life, resting by day in the woods, and repairing to marshes and bogs in the evening, to feed on worms and grubs which are obtained by thrusting their long beaks into the soft mud. Some of the woodcocks remain with us to breed, but the majority of them leave in March for their northern lands.

Hardly any insect life will be seen during the winter months, but on mild days dancing crowds of gnats and other allied species, and of the tiny winter midges, may be observed in the still air of sheltered spots. The beautiful hibernating butterflies already referred to will also be enticed from their hiding-places on any mild, sunny day, but only for a short time when the sun exerts its greatest power.

There are also several hibernating moths, mostly of rather dull greyish and brownish tints, but these, as a rule, are to be seen on the wing only in the dusk of mild evenings, for they rest during the daytime on tree-trunks, fences, etc., where they are usually rendered secure from the attacks of insectivorous birds by their protective colouring, which is often scarcely distinguishable from the sombre tints of their surroundings.

But, as regards these hibernating moths, there is one very interesting exception to the above rule. We refer to the beautiful humming-bird moth, which flies by day, and is roused from its slumbers on any mild, sunny day throughout the winter, to seek a meal of nectar from the few flowers that are still in bloom. It poises in the air beside a flower, its wings vibrating so rapidly that they are invisible, and producing a soft humming sound, while its long proboscis is thrust into the tube of the flower to suck up the sweet nectar. Any slight movement near at hand will cause it to dart away so rapidly that it is difficult to follow its motion, but it will almost invariably return to the same flower to resume its repast if no further danger threatens.

*Winter Moths: The Humming-Bird Moth (1), the Spring Usher and Female (2), the Early Moth (3), and the Small Eggar (4)*

Then, in addition to these hibernating insects, there are moths which emerge from the chrysalis state during the winter. These include the early-moth and the spring-usher, which appear on the wing in January; the small eggar, the pale brindled-beauty, and the dotted-border appearing in February; and the great oak-beauty and the March-moth late in the same month or early in

March. It is impossible to give detailed descriptions of these insects here, but photographs of some of them are included. The females of all these moths, with the exception of the small eggar and the great oak-beauty, are either quite wingless or have mere stumps of wings. Being unable to fly, they spend their time chiefly on the trunks of trees, where they run about in the evening, looking much more like spiders than moths.

*Winter Moths: The Pale Brindled Beauty (1), Dotted Border (2), Oak Beauty (3), and March Moth (4)*

# CHAPTER XXVI

# WINTER FLOWERS

ANY townsfolk seldom entertain the idea of a country ramble in the winter, and to them the suggestion of winter wild-flowers may seem strange. They look upon this season as the time to remain in town rather than to stray over the cold and bleak countryside, and are content to be ignorant of what may or may not be seen in wood, waste, and hedgerow.

Yet there are winter wild-flowers to be seen almost everywhere, and, though some of these may not be particularly showy, they are none the less interesting on that account, especially when we study them in their natural habitats.

There are a few flowers which bloom more or less throughout the year. They have their special season for appearing in abundance, but they linger on, and help, in their small way, to brighten the comparatively flowerless period.

On roadsides and in weedy wastes the flowering

stalks of the shepherd's-purse, bearing numerous triangular fruits, are tipped with tiny white blossoms; the chickweed displays its pretty white stars; the groundsel still bears its clusters of yellow flowers and its globular masses of tufted fruits; and the red dead-nettle carries its clusters of purple-red, lipped flowers in the axils of its heart-shaped leaves.

In sheltered places we may even see the pretty pink blossoms

*The Red Dead-Nettle*

of the Robert geranium or herb Robert up to the end of December, as well as the blue flowers of a species of speedwell, the former in hedge-banks and the latter in cultivated fields.

Then, soon after the new year opens, some of our earliest flowers begin to bloom. On moors and commons appears the golden yellow of the gorse or furze, and, in meadows

*The Herb Robert*

and thickets, the wild snowdrop. During February the henbit is in flower. This plant, with its purple-red blooms, is much like the red dead-nettle already mentioned, but its opposite leaves are stalkless, and the two forming each pair are so close together that they appear as one, with the stem of the plant running through it.

*The Henbit*

Now, also, the little strawberry-leaved cinquefoil will be found on almost every bank and hedge. Its leaves

and white flowers are so much like those of the wild strawberry that the plant is often mistaken for the latter, but its fruits are very small, dry, and seedlike. In fact the absence of succulent fruits on a plant so much like the strawberry plant has caused it to be named the "barren strawberry."

One of the most attractive features of copses

*The Strawberry-Leaved Cinquefoil*

*Flowers of the Hazel*

and hedgerows is certainly the dangling "lambs'-tails" of the hazel—dense, drooping clusters of tiny pollen-bearing flowers that yield little clouds of golden dust when shaken by the breeze on a fine sunny day. Lambs'-tails are more abundant in some years than in others; when they are unusually plentiful country-folk are wont to predict a generous crop of nuts in the following autumn. But lambs'-tails do not develop into nuts. They produce the pollen which is necessary for the fertilization of the fruiting flowers that present quite a different appearance.

If some twigs of the hazel bush be examined at the time when the lambs'-tails are in full bloom, some buds will be found very much like the ordinary "leaf-buds" in size and shape, but with a number of little deep-crimson filaments projecting from the tips. Each of these buds is a cluster of concealed fruiting flowers which have thrust out their crimson stigmas to catch the wind-borne pollen; each cluster, after fertilization, may produce from two or three to over a dozen nuts.

Before the winter is at an end several of our forest trees commence to bloom. On the banks of streams and in other wet places we may see the alder tree in flower about the end of February.

In this case, too, we have two distinct kinds of flower-clusters—long, drooping catkins of pollen-bearing flowers, much like those of the hazel, and clusters of fruiting flowers that look like small, green fir-cones. Both alder and hazel produce their flowers before the

*Flowers of the Alder*

leaves appear; this is advantageous to the trees, for the pollen is dispersed by the wind, and, in the absence of foliage, the fruiting flowers have a better chance of catching some of the fertilizing grains.

On a dry, breezy day in late February thick clouds of yellowish-white dust are blown from the branches of some yew trees. This is the pollen set free from little clusters of flowers which occupy the angles formed by leaves and stem. We say some yew trees, because, in the case of the yew, the pollen-bearing and the fruiting flowers generally grow on separate trees, so that it is necessary for the pollen to be wafted from one tree to another before fertilization can take place. Under such circumstances there is an enormous waste of pollen, since the trees producing the pollen are often very far from those which bear the fruiting flowers, and it is to compensate for this unavoidable waste during transfer that such enormous quantities are formed. The distribution of pollen by the wind is always a wasteful

237

*Flowers of the Elm*

process, even when the two kinds of flowers are borne on the same plant; for that reason the wind-pollinated species always produce more pollen than those which arrange for their pollination through the agency of insects.

At about the same time the tips of the elm branches begin to assume a somewhat fluffy appearance, more especially towards the top of the tree. This is due to the opening of the flowers. Sometimes the flowers appear on branches that are within easy reach; they are in dense clusters, and of a reddish colour. There is only one kind of flower on the elm, for stamens (which produce pollen) and ovary (which forms the fruit) both exist in each separate blossom.

A little later in the season the purple willow and the white poplar are in bloom. In both of these trees the two kinds of flowers are on separate plants; the two kinds are so different in appearance, in each case, that the trees bearing them might be mistaken for distinct species.

The pollen-bearing flowers of the purple willow are in closely-packed catkins, about an inch long, and each little flower has stamens and a little purple-tipped scale with short, silky hair. The fruiting catkins are also silky, but each flower consists only of an ovary and its little scale.

In the white poplar the pollen-bearing catkins are often three or four inches long, and each flower has several purple stamens, while the fruiting catkins are much shorter. Both are clothed with silky hairs.

Before the winter is quite over, many of the so-called spring flowers make their appearance, especially in sheltered places and on banks facing south.

On walls and dry banks is the whitlow-grass, with its tiny rosette of leaves close to the root, and its stalks of little white flowers with four deeply-cleft petals. This plant seldom grows more than two or three inches high.

*The Whitlow-Grass*

Damp, shady banks are often richly decorated with the glossy heart-shaped leaves and buttercup-like flowers of the lesser celandine; shady river-banks and marshy places have large patches completely carpeted with the beautiful golden saxifrage.

Before February is out, if the season is very mild, the favourite primrose and sweet violet expand their blossoms on shady banks, frequently in company with the lovely wood-anemone, and above them often appear

*The Lesser Celandine*     *Golden Saxifrage*

the snowy flowers of the sloe or blackthorn, thickly covering their leafless twigs. In the woods are the brown flowers of the hairy woodrush, whose grasslike leaves are fringed with long, silky hairs, and, in meadows and waste places, the earliest of the grasses—the annual meadow-grass—in full bloom.

*The Hairy Woodrush*     *The Annual Meadow Grass*

# CHAPTER XXVII

# EVERGREENS

HROUGHOUT the winter months we are naturally attracted by those trees and shrubs which remain in leaf, since their dark-green foliage renders them very conspicuous when all the neighbouring trees are bare. Although some of these evergreens are too well known to need any description, particularly those which are so popular for Christmas decorations, yet we propose to devote a short chapter dealing with the chief features of evergreen trees generally, with such descriptions and illustrations as may enable all the principal species to be identified.

In the first place the evergreen trees are specially adapted to withstand the winter frosts and storms. Their wood is so tough and elastic that the branches are not easily broken by boisterous winds. Their leaves are generally thick and of a tough, leathery nature; the skin or epidermis, exceedingly thin and delicate on most leaves, is usually very much thicker in the case of evergreens; the outer walls of the external layer of cells are much thickened to prevent undue loss of moisture at a time when the roots are unable to extract much water from the soil, because they are rendered inactive by the low temperature of the ground.

The leaves themselves are inactive during the cold weather, and are compelled to take their winter rest. In fact several important chemical changes take place within the leaves to enable them better to withstand the low temperature to which they are exposed, and although these changes do not cause very marked alterations in the general appearance of the foliage, yet to them is due the darker colour, often a bluish green, assumed by the leaves on the approach of winter.

Three of the British evergreen trees belong to the cone-bearing or naked-seeded trees. These are the common pine, the yew, and the juniper. The first of these, known properly as the Scots pine, is sometimes confused with one or more of the numerous pines that have been introduced into this country, but may be distinguished by its leaves, which are needle-like, seldom more than two inches long, and arranged in pairs, and also by the form of its cone. The cones take about eighteen or twenty months to ripen, and thus we

*A Group of Pine Trees*

242

find the fruits of two successive years on the tree at the same time.

*An Old Yew*

The sombre, densely-branched yew can hardly be mistaken for any other evergreen tree, for it can be distinguished easily, at a considerable distance, by its very dark foliage and its spreading habit. It is a very slow grower, and lives to a great age, probably more than two thousand years. The leaves are very narrow, glossy above, seldom more than three-quarters of an inch long, and spread in one plane on the two opposite sides of the twig. We have already observed that this tree flowers during the winter, and its fruits are described in an earlier chapter.

The juniper is usually a shrub rather than a tree, and, though generally very small, sometimes reaches a height of ten or fifteen feet. It does not appear to be well known to most country ramblers, although it is common in

*A Twig of the Juniper*

many hilly districts. The leaves are very narrow, not more than half an inch long, slightly curved, and arranged in whorls of three. The bush bears very small flowers in May, and its berry-like fruits are not ripe till the following summer.

It may appear strange that the juniper should be classed with the cone-bearing trees, for its fruits are very different in appearance from those of pines and firs, but the one or two hard seeds in the "berry" are naked in the sense that they are not enclosed in an ovary, for the succulent mass around them is formed by the union of a few fleshy scales which correspond with the woody scales of a typical cone.

A large number of evergreen cone-bearing trees have been introduced into Britain, but they are to be found principally in parks and plantations rather than in the open country. They comprise a few firs, of which the spruce and silver firs are best known, some pines, including the stone pine, Austrian pine, Chili pine, etc., and a few species of cedar and cypress. These are well worth study, but we have no space to deal with them here.

Coming back to our British evergreens, we must first

give some attention to the ivy, the general appearance of which is so well known that we should pass it over with the briefest notice were it not for its interesting habits. It is so variable in build and habit that one might suppose there were several distinct species of the climber instead of only one. As we see it climbing the oak trees and old buildings it is vastly different from the same plant when creeping along the ground or winding amongst the herbage of hedge-banks. In the former situations its leaves are large and of a bright-green colour, but in the hedgerow they are much smaller, more variable in form, and fre-

*Stem of Ivy on the Bole of the Oak*

quently variegated with a number of beautiful tints. Also, while the climbing ivy usually bears flowers and fruits in profusion, the trailing plant seldom does.

As long as the ivy stems have a surface above them to which they can cling, the tree spends its energies in soaring upwards rather than in producing flowers and fruit. The climbing stems always bear five-angled leaves which turn their upper surfaces towards the strongest light, and arrange themselves in such a manner as to catch the maximum of the sun's rays.

But when the ivy twigs can no longer climb, either

because they have reached the top of the supporting structure or because the surface of that structure near them is already completely covered, they extend themselves upwards or outwards, for a foot or two only, and at the same time change their mode of growth in a remarkable manner. They no longer give rise to five-angled leaves turned all one way, but produce undivided leaves, smaller in size, and facing all directions. Then, in October, these free, bushy twigs produce umbels of yellowish-green flowers which, in their turn, give rise to smooth, green berries that ripen to black during the present season.

The holly is another well-known and favourite evergreen concerning which a description would be superfluous, but which has a habit that is much too interesting to be passed over. We are all familiar with the stiff, sharp spines which project from the margins of the leaves. These serve to protect the foliage from the attacks of herbivorous creatures. The young leaves, which are produced on new twigs in spring and early summer, are much softer than the old leaves, and their spines are not so formidable. This young foliage would be eaten largely by browsing animals were it not that, at the time, green food is particularly abundant, so much so that the holly and other shrubs receive little attention. But later in the year, when green herbage is getting scarce, the holly is well protected, for now its spines are rigid and defiant.

Now examine the foliage of holly bushes that have reached a height of several feet, and you will almost invariably find that while the lower leaves are well defended by the usual spines, the latter become less in number, on each leaf, towards the top; the topmost branches of all generally bear leaves that have but few spines or none at all. So the bush produces its weapons of defence in abundance where they are necessary,

*Twigs of the Holly*

and but few or none where the leaves are beyond the reach of browsing animals.

We must include one other well-known evergreen—the mistletoe—on the ground of an interesting habit that may not be thoroughly understood. The mistletoe is a parasitic plant, feeding on the sap of the tree on which it grows. Undoubtedly birds, especially thrushes, are responsible for the distribution of its seeds. The birds devour mistletoe berries, and deposit the undigested seeds on the bark of trees. When these seeds germinate, the young plants send "sinkers" to the living tissues of the tree for the purpose of extracting the sap. The mistletoe flowers in the spring, and its fruits (berries) are ripe at the end of the year. Some mistletoe tufts never produce berries. The reason is that pollen flowers and fruiting flowers are quite distinct, and are borne on separate plants.

Hitherto we have spoken almost exclusively of evergreen shrubs and trees, but, quite apart from our forest trees and our numerous shrubs, the countryside is green almost everywhere all through the winter. Pastures, meadows, banks, waysides, and waste places all still have green as the predominant colour. This is due to the abundance of perennial plants whose foliage does not completely die down on the approach of winter. Many of the grasses are perpetually green, and although the flowering stalks and upper foliage of perennials die down at the fall of the year, large numbers of these plants retain a cluster of green leaves, close to the ground, throughout the winter.

## CHAPTER XXVIII

# FROST AND SNOWSTORM

EW countryside scenes are more beautiful than those displayed after a night of hard white frost, and after a moderately heavy fall of snow.

In the first case, although the vegetation is not completely hidden by the crystal growth that clothes it, yet the landscape has an almost uniform appearance of whiteness. The general effect is pleasing, but the chief beauties of the frost, it seems to us, are revealed when we closely examine the exquisite forms of the little crystals on stems, leaves, and other objects, and the manner in which they are arranged.

The crystals sometimes completely cover the upper surfaces of leaves, but are usually much more thickly disposed, and of longer growth, on the margins. Often they are slender, prismatic needles, with smooth surfaces that reflect the bright rays of the rising sun, glistening like so many diamonds; at other times they assume the form of a flocculent rime which scarcely

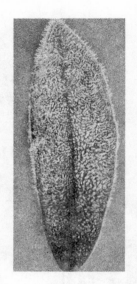

*Frost on Privet Leaves*      *Frost on a Leaf of the Rhododendron*

reveals a crystalline structure unless we examine it with a magnifying lens.

Walking over grass-land on a sharp frosty morning, we hear a distinct crunching sound with every footstep, for not only do we crush the icy crystals fringing the blades, but the blades themselves are rendered rigid by the freezing of the sap within them. They have also lost, for the time, their natural elasticity, and remain lying close to the ground where they are trodden down, until the warmth of the sun's rays has thawed the sap within their cells.

Much more noisy is the tread as we walk on the thick carpet of fallen leaves in the woodland path, for the leaves, although dead, usually contain a certain amount of moisture absorbed from rain, dew, or the moist ground on which they lie, and it is the freezing of this moisture which renders them so brittle. Note how the crystals of hoar-frost are disposed on the upper surfaces of these dead leaves. Some of the latter still retain their natural crinkles, determined by the arrangement of their veins, and others have become more or less crinkled in drying. The frost lies thickest on all the projecting ridges and margins, while the furrows, more sheltered from the frost-giving breeze, are lightly covered.

Frost and dew are formed both in the same manner. In fact, frost may be termed "frozen dew." When air, laden with moisture, comes in contact with a colder object, some of the invisible moisture is condensed on the surface of that object, giving rise to a deposit of dew, but if the object on which the moisture is deposited is at a temperature below the freezing-point, then each particle is frozen as it settles, and a continuation of the process leads to the gradual growth of the crystals of frost.

The heaviest deposits of both dew and frost occur on clear nights when there is a *gentle* breeze. It is on clear nights only that the ground and the vegetation become sufficiently cold to condense much moisture, for a cloudy atmosphere acts like a blanket over the earth, preventing the free radiation of heat from the latter. Then as to the other factor mentioned, it is necessary for the air to be in motion in order to bring renewed supplies of moisture against the cold objects on the earth; yet if the breeze is strong, it passes by those cold objects too quickly to permit the air being sufficiently cooled to cause any condensation.

The appearance of the countryside after a snow-storm is very different from that due to a sharp frost. Now a dazzling whiteness prevails everywhere, with scarcely a bare object to break the continuity of the snowy garment. All low herbage is completely covered. Branches and tree-trunks are all clothed above and on the sides exposed to the wind. Evergreens are apparently crushed by the weight they have to bear, and the lower branches of yews, pines, and firs are often bowed to the ground. Should the atmosphere be clear, the bright rays of the sun are reflected from the smooth faces of the snow crystals, and all around us is a brilliant scintillation of the minute starry gems.

On the moorland and in the open field it is interesting to observe the footprints of the numerous wild creatures which have left their tracks in the freshly-fallen snow. Here we see the track of the rabbit on its nocturnal search for food or its mates—a series of footprints in clusters of four, two longer ones some inches apart, and two smaller near the middle of the track. The former are a little behind the latter if the creature was advancing with slow and deliberate step, but outside or even in front if the rabbit was "on the run." There is the track of a pheasant—alternate footprints, with the impressions of the three long front toes quite distinct, and often a continuous line between them, drawn by the long tail as it lightly brushed the loose surface of the snow. Then the footprints of small birds are quite numerous, and sometimes we come across the alternating impressions of the feet of a fox, with a medial trail where the surface snow has been lightly swept by the creature's "brush." Many a time have we traced a wild creature to its haunt by following its track in a recent fall of snow.

Snowstorms are very variable in their nature, being greatly influenced by the atmospheric conditions prevailing at the time. If the air is very keen the snow is always perfectly dry and powdery. Each particle is a perfect six-sided crystal if the air is calm, but a little rounded, floccular, crystalline mass in a high wind. If, however, the snow passes through air that is only a little above the freezing temperature, the crystals are partially melted and, in their wet condition, they unite together into confused masses or flakes.

Take a block of ice, such as a portion of a thick icicle, break it, and then fit the two surfaces of the fracture together again. If the air is very cold, and the ice consequently dry, the two pieces will not unite. But if the temperature of the air is above the freezing-point, and the two pieces of ice wet on account of the thawing at the surface, they will immediately freeze together. This little experiment will partially explain how it is that the snow crystals can unite to form flakes only when the air is mild.

Many persons have never seen the varied, exquisite forms of perfect crystals of snow. They have, no doubt, seen enlarged representations of them in book illustrations, and it is probable that the expression "as seen under a microscope" has led them to suppose that it is possible to examine the crystals only when aided by some powerful magnifier. Such is not the case. Let the fine snow of a keen, calm day fall on a dark coat-sleeve; the crystals are often so large that their general forms can be distinguished well without any optical aid, and even the details of their structure with the help of a good hand-lens. The examination must be conducted out of doors or in a very cold room, and care must be taken to prevent the warm breath from melting the crystals during observation.

As milder weather approaches, the snow slowly melts. The ground beneath, if free of vegetation, previously pulverised by the recent frosts, is soon saturated with the water of the thawing snow above it, and we get that unpleasant, cold, muddy slush which always follows.

It sometimes appears as if an enormous quantity of water is produced by the melting of the snows, but the volume of water is very small compared with that of the snow yielding it. If you collect falling snow in a cylindrical vessel, measure its depth, and then take it indoors to melt, you will find that the depth of the water produced is only about one-twelfth that of the snow, or even less. We have already said that snow is very variable in its nature, but, as a rule, twelve to fourteen inches of snow are equivalent to one inch of rain. It is seldom that we get an inch or more of rain in one day, and we certainly do not frequently get its equivalent in snow all within twenty-four hours.

The gradual disappearance of the snow on herbage, shrubs, and trees is more interesting. The herbage, released from its burden, responds to the welcome rays of the sun, and is none the worse for its temporary repression. It has been kept warmer by the mantle of snow, which has prevented the warmth of the soil from radiating into space, and it looks fresher than before. The shrubs, too, gradually recover themselves as they become free, and the boughs of evergreen trees are brought back to their former positions by the elasticity of their wood as the melting snow slides and drips from their leaves.

CPSIA information can be obtained
at www.ICGtesting.com
Printed in the USA
JSHW020931050423
39830JS00006B/43